D1172470

Saint & Greavsie's

FUNNY OLD GAMES

sphere

SPHERE

First published in Great Britain in 2008 by Sphere

A CIP catalogue record for this book
is available from the British Library.

ISBN 978-1-84744-251-2

Typeset in Melior by M Rules
Printed and bound in Great Britain by
Clays Ltd, St Ives plc

Papers used by Sphere are natural, renewable and recyclable
products made from wood grown in sustainable forests and certified
in accordance with the rules of the Forest Stewardship Council.

Sphere
An imprint of
Little, Brown Book Group
100 Victoria Embankment
London EC4Y 0DY

An Hachette Livre UK Company
www.hachettelivre.co.uk

www.littlebrown.co.uk

To the memory of our old mates Bobby Moore and Jim Baxter, who were always good for a laugh as well as being footballing geniuses

Contents

Acknowledgements

Saint and Greavsie wish to thank the Sphere team, and in particular Adam Strange, for their expert help in getting this book into the net. We are indebted to Iain Hunt and Helen Pisano for their editing skills and Michael Giller for his safety-net checking work on the hundreds of sports anecdotes. Thanks to Peter Cotton for a perfectly tailored jacket, and to Kezia Storr of PA Photos for her help on picture research. Most of all, thanks to all our pals in and around the sports world who have so willingly helped us with their memories. You are too many to mention, but you know who you are! And, of course, thanks to our old mate, sports historian Norman Giller, for pulling it all together, just for a laugh. A final thanks to Terry and Freda Baker of A1 Sporting Speakers who made it all possible. Most of all thanks to YOU for buying the book. Enjoy!

Kick-Off

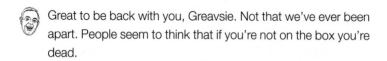 Great to be back with you, Greavsie. Not that we've ever been apart. People seem to think that if you're not on the box you're dead.

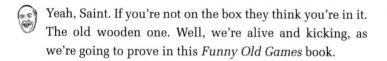 Yeah, Saint. If you're not on the box they think you're in it. The old wooden one. Well, we're alive and kicking, as we're going to prove in this *Funny Old Games* book.

Correct. We're both hooked on all sports, and this book gives us the chance to have a good-natured dig at today's so-called superstars.

Good-natured? Blimey, Saint, don't tell me you've gone soft on me. Tell it like it is. We're going to put the boot in . . . just for a laugh.

The point I'm making is that people think because we were professional footballers that's the only sport we're interested in.

True, Saint. Like me, you follow most of the major sports. In fact, it might surprise a lot of people to know that my favourite sport these days is not football, but rugby union.

Come off it, Greavsie. Rugby has got a lot going for it, but football's still the king. It's just that they're doing their best to make a mess of it.

 There are players picking up a hundred grand a week who are like pickpockets, stealing money from the fans. I'm not going to name names 'cos I don't want to make libel lawyers Sue, Grabbitt and Run any richer. But you know who they are, Saint, the same as I do.

 Aye, they come off the pitch at the end with jerseys as dry as when they went on. My dear old manager Bill Shankly would have called them the Idle Rich. But there are some exceptional players like Ronaldo, Fabregas, Fernando Torres and Didier Drogba, who've brought new skills and standards to the Premier League.

 Drogba was hardly exceptional in the Champions League final against Man United. If I'd been his team-mate, I'd have given him a right mouthful for getting himself sent off in such a ridiculous way. And how about Nicklearse Anelka? He bottled it and left John Terry to take the vital fifth penalty. Terry was known as Mister Chelsea, now he'll be remembered as Mister Penalty.

 I confess that I wasn't keen on taking penalties, but it was not such an important part of the game in our day. The shoot-outs were not introduced until we'd hung up our boots. There was an even worse lottery in our playing days. I was in the Liverpool side that reached the semi-final of the European Cup in 1965 on the flip of a disc after we had finished deadlocked with Cologne. Our skipper Ron Yeats tossed the disc – red on one side for Liverpool, white on the other for Cologne – and it stuck on its side in the mud. It was real Monty Python stuff. He tossed again and it came down red. Another time we lost a match on a toss of a coin, and when our captain told Bill Shankly he had called tails, Shanks said: 'Och, ye should have called heads.'

 Whichever officials thought of that way of settling a match were a load of tossers. They are the sort of people whose egos we'll be looking to prick in the following pages. Our brief from our publisher is to make people laugh, and I think we should manage that between us.

 Aye, we can pass on all those funny sports stories we've collected over the years and we have a load of anecdotes about the old *Saint and Greavsie* show when we used to pull in bigger audiences than any other daytime show. I think it fair to say we pioneered mixing humour with fact in football.

 Yeah, but now you have to be able to boil an egg, hang a bit of paper or plant a bloody daffodil to get on the box. You can't switch on the telly without seeing so-called celebrity chefs, decorators, dancers or wannabe pop stars filling our screens.

 Careful, Greavsie. You're sounding like a grumpy old footballer. Let's stick to the funny stuff. Anybody looking for a pattern to this book will find themselves in a bit of a maze. We're just going to go where our memories and opinions take us. Hopefully we'll raise a few laughs on the way.

 Let's kick off our collection of funny sports stories by doing what comes naturally, Saint . . . talking a load of balls . . .

1 A LOAD OF BALLS

 This is where we tell off-beat stories about all ball games, Greavsie. That gives us lots of scope. You go first.

 Remember that bird, Erica Roe, who did a famous head-line-hitting streak at Twickenham? She was an impressively built girl. Big Bill Beaumont, who was then England skipper, told me that he was standing with his back to her, so didn't see her starting to run the length of the field. He said first he knew of it was when scrum-half Steve Smith shouted, 'Hey, Bill, there's a bird just run on with your bum on her chest.'

 They were real characters in rugby then. It's gone down in folk-lore how England were celebrating a rare win in Paris about the same season as the Erica Roe streak. During the post-match banquet, the teams were presented with complimentary bottles of aftershave. England forward Maurice Colclough emptied the contents of his bottle into an ice-bucket and replaced it with water. He drank it in front of the England prop Colin Smart, convincing him it was vintage wine.

Colin then copied Colclough by swallowing a bottle of the real thing. Not a smart thing to do. He ended up in hospital having his stomach pumped. Joker Steve Smith commented: 'Colin was in a bad way, but his breath smelt lovely.'

 From then on Colin was known to one and all as Brut! I did my fair share of drinking, Saint, but I never got round to trying aftershave. It's sure to make you stinking drunk.

Booze can make you do potty things. Ask England's most capped goalkeeper Peter Shilton! He was arrested for drink driving after being found at 5 a.m. in a country lane with, so it was reported, somebody's else's wife in his car. Suddenly her husband arrived on the scene, and as Shilts – caught with his trousers down – drove away like the clappers he crashed into a lamppost (he had no idea whether it was the near post or the far one). He admitted 'taking a lady for a meal' and was heavily fined and banned from driving for fifteen months. He then had to put up with teasing terrace chants of 'Shilton, Shilton, where's your wife?'

 Up on Merseyside we still laugh at the unbelievable boozy night Everton's Peter Beagrie had in Spain. Everton were on a pre-season tour, and Beagrie over-indulged following a game with Real Sociedad. It was the early hours of the morning when he arrived back at the team hotel on the back of a motorcycle on which a friendly Spaniard had given him a lift. Banging drunkenly on the locked hotel's front door, he couldn't rouse the night porter.

Beagrie, legless of course, grabbed the Spaniard's bike, rode it up the hotel steps (as you do) . . . and straight through a plate-glass window. Guess what, Greavsie. It was the wrong hotel! Beagrie was taken off to hospital to have loads of stitches in lacerations. When the story got out, the rest of the football world was in stitches.

 One more booze story. When England won the Ashes in 2005, Freddie Flintoff and Matthew Hoggard were, to put it mildly, sozzled by the time they got to Downing Street for an official team reception. Freddie went into Number 10 with the word TWAT scrawled on his forehead, and Hoggy called Prime Minister Tony Blair a knob to his face. There had not been such scenes at Number 10 since the last Cabinet meeting.

One of the players peed in the Downing Street garden. Freddie denies that it was him, but I've been trusted with the name of the culprit and I told him at a recent sportsmen's dinner that he should have directed his pee towards Mr Blair . . .

 No politics, please Greavsie. But if you're going to talk about peeing then former world snooker champion Alex Higgins has to take the crown. He got banned from one tournament for urinating in his dressing-room sink! Then he went one better, relieving himself in a flowerpot during the 1976 World Championships. When accused, Alex said it was a plant. I made that last bit up!

 Reminds me of the time I was pissed on. England were playing Brazil in the quarter-final of the World Cup in Chile in 1962. A stray dog invaded the pitch during the first half. It led a posse of ball boys and players a dance before I went down on all fours to capture it. He seemed very relieved as I handed him to an official. So relieved, in fact, that he rewarded me by pissing all the way down the front of my England shirt and shorts.

In those days there were no second kits provided, so I couldn't change at half-time and ponged all through the game. Garrincha, an animal-loving country boy who kept, among other things, fifty birds in his village home, fell in love with the stray. He saw the dog as a lucky omen because of the unbelievable game he – Garrincha, not the dog! – had against us, and took it home to Brazil with him.

After their 3-1 victory, he told reporters that he was going to name the dog after me, 'Yimmy Greaves'. He was barking mad.

Funniest dog story I've heard is when your old Tottenham team-mate Frank Saul was having a bit of a nightmare playing in a game at Queen's Park Rangers. A dog came scampering on to the pitch, and while players were trying to catch it somebody shouted from the terraces: 'Leave the dog on, take Saul off!'

Frank was a much underrated player and scored the second goal for us in our 2-1 victory over Chelsea in the 1967 FA Cup final. I was marked that day – marked being the operative word – by the notorious 'Chopper' Harris, who would have kicked anything that moved for a win bonus. Ron's a good buddy of mine these days, and often joins me on my road show. He tells the lovely story of when the Duke of Edinburgh was watching him play at Stamford Bridge.

The Duke asked the then Chelsea chairman Brian Mears why he was called Chopper. Just as the question was out of his mouth, Ron chopped down an opponent with one of his scything tackles. 'Oh,' said the Duke, quite disappointed. 'Now I know.' He thought it might have been because of the way Chopper was hung.

When I used to play against Chopper – the experience is a bruise on my memory – he used to stay closer to me than sticking plaster. I said to him during one game, 'I bet if I go for a sh** you'll be there to wipe my arse.'

'No, I won't,' he said. 'But I'll be there at the door waiting for you when you come out.'

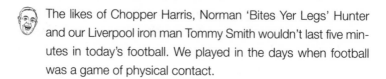

The likes of Chopper Harris, Norman 'Bites Yer Legs' Hunter and our Liverpool iron man Tommy Smith wouldn't last five minutes in today's football. We played in the days when football was a game of physical contact.

Yeah, players now go down as if they're shot if anybody tries to make a proper old-style tackle. If we'd played under today's no-tackling rules, Saint, I reckon we would have doubled our goal output. Chopper Harris, Norman Hunter, Tommy Smith and Co would have seen more red cards than Paul Daniels.

Steady, Greavsie. We're back to being Grumpy Old Footballers again. Talking of Tommy Smith, I was playing for Liverpool in a pre-season friendly in Germany when he started mowing down opponents with his famed and feared tackling. 'Friendly' was not in his vocabulary on the football pitch. The German referee felt moved to come into the dressing room at half-time and forewarned our manager Bill Shankly in broken English: 'Smith – number four – one bad tackle more – off!'

Shanks digested this and replied in broken Scottish: 'Smith – if he off – *everybody* off!'

Tommy was a real hard nut. He would have kicked his granny if it meant stopping the ball going into the net. Once when I was playing for Spurs at Anfield he came up to me just before the kick-off and handed me a piece of paper. It was the menu for the local Liverpool hospital!

His reputation was such that players used to swallow it against him even before a ball was kicked. I remember him once asking Shanks how he wanted him to play against one of those all-show ball-playing types. Shanks said: 'Just go and stand next to him.' The opponent got rid of the ball like a hot potato and didn't dare try any of his fancy tricks. Here's a mind-blowing fact for you. In more than six hundred games for Liverpool Tommy was sent off only once, and that was for dissent.

That does amaze me. Perhaps the referees were frightened of him, too? The Anfield fans used to throw raw meat to him while he was warming up.

A policeman with a pushbike tried to arrest Tommy once after a match for using the f-word during the game, in the hearing of spectators. Shanks told the copper, 'F*** off, or I'll let the tyres down on your bike!' If they arrested footballers for swearing during a game, Greavsie, they would finish up playing two-a-side.

F*** knows, Saint! Best swearing story involved that great Fulham character Tosh Chamberlain. He was sent off for calling the referee a c***. Tosh protested his innocence, saying: 'But I wasn't talking to you, ref. I was calling Johnny Haynes a c***, and I can do that 'cos he's on my side!'

Who'd be a referee or an umpire, Saint? They just can't win. I'd like to see more referees with personality. Too many of them are robots. They could learn about communicating with the players from that unique cricket character Dickie Bird. He told me a great yarn when we met on the after-dinner speaking circuit.

Dickie said that one of his favourite players was Dennis Lillee, arguably the finest of all fast bowlers. He was fiercely competitive, but Dickie said even in the intense heat of a Test match he'd find time for some banter. Once, after Dickie had turned down his loud lbw appeal, Dennis told him: 'I think your eyesight's going, Dickie.'

'Oh no,' replied Dickie, 'it's YOUR eyesight that's going. I'm the ice-cream seller.'

I got another Dickie Bird story from Sir Ian Botham when I joined him on one of his charity walks. Both said that towards the end of his career, when he was combining cricket with pantomime appearances, he rapped a batsman on the pads and shouted: 'Owzat!'

Dickie responded with a panto-style shout: 'Oh no he isn't!'

Ian reckoned he got some of the worst reviews of any panto star. He appeared in *Babes in the Wood* and one critic wrote: 'Botham was more wooden than any tree in the forest.'

 I've got a Dickie Bird story, too. In the early days of mobile telephones he was standing in the middle umpiring a match at Northampton when Allan Lamb came in to bat. He handed Dickie one of the new-fangled phones and said, 'Meant to leave this in the dressing room. Look after it for me, Dickie.'

Those were the days when the mobile phone was the size of a brick. Five minutes later the telephone rang, and Dickie jumped a foot in the air. Lambie, at the other end, shouted: 'Answer it, Dickie, and tell them to ring back.'

Dickie did as he was asked, and fumed when he found it

was Ian Botham on the line asking him the score, and if he could speak to Lambie.

 Dickie told me he said to Both: 'Hang on. He won't be in for long.'

Lambie was always playing tricks on his mate Dickie. Once during the World Cup in India, Dickie was confined to bed with a tummy bug. The hotel he was in was ringed with armed security forces because of political unrest.

His bedside phone rang, and it was Lambie in sympathetic mood: 'I've got something that I think will cure you. All right if I come to your room?'

'That's kind of you, Allan,' Dickie said, forgetting he was

Dickie Bird gives it the finger in front of the statue erected in his hometown of Barnsley (Anna Gowthorpe/PA Wire).

talking to the king of the leg pullers. 'My door's unlocked. Come on up.'

When Lambie arrived he was accompanied by a squad of six rifle-carrying soldiers he had rounded up from the troops outside. He lined them up around Dickie's bed and said: 'Okay, let's put the poor bugger out of his misery. Ready! Aim! Fire!'

Dickie said the laugh did him good, but he was not laughing another time at breakfast in a Northampton hotel when the newspaper he was reading caught fire, and he had to throw his coffee over it to put it out. He blew his top when he found Lambie crouching under his table with a lighter in hand!

 It didn't end there, Greavsie. Dickie was umpiring at Old Trafford when Lancashire were playing Northants. As he and his colleague, Ray Julian, went to leave their dressing room they found the door had been locked from the outside. Suddenly smoke started coming under the door. The umpires were just about to panic when an Old Trafford groundsman burst in with a fire extinguisher and put out the small fire outside the door.

When Dickie got to the middle he found Lambie and his Northants team-mates rolling about laughing.

As they came off at the end of the session, Lambie put an arm around Dickie's shoulders and apologised for the latest prank. Dickie forgave him, and warned him to stop the jokes because he thought it was getting out of hand. They shook hands and Allan vowed to behave in future.

Leaving the ground at the end of the match, Dickie went to the car park where he found his motor minus wheels and up on bricks. Scrawled on the windscreen was the message: 'Have a safe journey home, Dickie. See you next season!'

I'll tell you the hardest of the ball games I've played, Saint – squash. I used to think I was quite good at it, until I went on court with one of the world's greatest ever players, Jonah Barrington. He moved around the court so fast it was as if there were two of him, and when he hit the ball it was just a blur. Gary Newbon said to Central TV viewers that Jonah had a whale of a time with me.

It was Jonah who told me about the game in which his opponent farted loudly as he reached for a wall shot. Jonah laughed so much he failed to get the return back. 'It was the first time,' Jonah said, 'that a point had been won on an inside court that was wind assisted!'

 Talking of wind assistance reminds me of that great Everton character Sandy Brown, a legend on Merseyside. When Peter 'Hot Shot' Lorimer was getting loads of publicity for having the hardest shot in football, Sandy boasted he packed a harder one. He was told that Lorimer's shot-speed had been timed at more than seventy miles per hour, and Sandy insisted he could shoot faster.

Goalkeeper Gordon West, a great wind-up merchant, saw the opening for a prank, and told Sandy that he had thought of a way of timing his shooting power. Westie said he would set up a controlled test at the club's Bellefield training ground.

The next day Sandy was stationed at the halfway line on the training pitch, a ball at his feet, and with Gordon revving up his car alongside the touchline but back by the corner flag. Sandy was told to delay his kick until Gordon's car had reached the halfway line, by which time he would be motoring at seventy miles per hour. If Sandy could get the ball to reach the goal area ahead of the car it would be proof that he could shoot the ball faster than seventy mph.

They had half a dozen goes at it before Sandy at last got the ball to arrive ahead of the car, by which time Gordon could hardly drive for laughing. Sandy was just congratulating himself when Alex Young held up a flapping handkerchief and announced Sandy's fastest effort couldn't count because it had been wind assisted. It was only then that Sandy realised he had been, so to speak, taken for a ride.

 Another hilarious Sandy Brown story is when he went to New York on a summer tour with Everton. Most of the other players were sitting in the bar at the posh Waldorf Astoria when Sandy made his entrance, wearing an immaculate white jacket, bow tie, silk pocket handkerchief, and sunglasses. He was a clone of James Bond. He sauntered to the bar, the epitome of cool, and said to the impressed barman in his best Sean Connery voice: 'Scotch on the rocks . . . no ice!'

 I heard a lovely story when I was in New York back in the seventies. Joe Namath was the idolised quarterback with the New York Jets. He was on a par with Pele and Muhammad Ali in the hero stakes, and they reckoned only O. J. Simpson could match him. Namath had played in the first match on Astroturf as American football started to make the switch from traditional grass surfaces. At the press conference following the game on the synthetic surface, he was asked: 'What's the difference between grass and Astroturf?'

'Well,' drawled Joe, 'I can't rightly say 'cos I've never smoked Astroturf.'

 I remember meeting William Perry, the Fridge, when he came over to play American football for the London Monarchs. He stood six foot two, weighed twenty-five stone and he wore the biggest Super Bowl ring in history. I could have got two of my fingers into it. When I asked him if he would consider playing rugby without all the padding they use in American football he said: 'I may look dumb, man. But I ain't *that* dumb!'

 While we're talking about big American sportsmen, how about – and this is a true story – the six-foot-nine-inch tall former basketball star who fell on hard times. For legal reasons, let's call him Butch. He held up a store in his neighbourhood, armed with a gun and wearing a poorly fitted mask. The store-owner recognised the one-time local hero and said: 'Don't do this, Butch. Put the gun down.' Butch was shown on CCTV saying: 'It ain't me, man. Just hand over the money.'

 When the Michael Jordan-led USA team won the basketball gold medal in the 1984 LA Olympics, their coach Bob Knight got a big laugh after a comfortable preliminary-round victory over China. He said: 'It was a lot of fun playing the Chinese, but an hour later, we wanted to play them again.'

 My top ball game, as you know, Greavsie, is the one that Scotland gave to the world – golf, of course. I never thought I'd ever see a better player than Jack Nicklaus, but Tiger Woods is well on his way to beating his Majors record.

When Tiger first started winning everything in sight Bill Clinton was President. The Monica Lewinsky scandal was at its peak, and the story went that after Tiger had won the US Masters the President rang to congratulate him and said: 'Why not come over for a foursome . . . and maybe we could also play a little golf sometime.'

 A story that sums up Tiger's extraordinary 'feel' for golf comes from a Nike contact of mine. He told me that Nike

Golf once sent Tiger a batch of five prototype drivers to test out. He reported back that he liked the heaviest one best. This caused confusion and consternation among the Nike designers, who believed that each driver weighed exactly the same. They collected the clubs and performed additional tests, and found that the driver Tiger preferred indeed outweighed the others – by an amount equivalent to two dollar bills!

 His caddy, Steve Williams from New Zealand, is the highest paid sportsman in Kiwi sport! He has become a multi-millionaire just carrying the great man's clubs, and his earnings if he were a tour player would put him in the top bracket. He earns more from a year on the course with Tiger than many people in a lifetime. It is just another sign of the phenomenal earning power of Tiger Woods.

 Even Tiger can see that his legions of fans sometimes go overboard with their support. During one of the US Opens he took a comfort break, and as he came out of the Portaloo the fans started applauding him. 'Hell,' said Tiger, 'I'm now getting clapped 'cos I'm potty trained.'

 Mentioning the loo, Greavsie, did you see that story about Portsmouth fullback Glen Johnson getting fined for stealing a toilet seat from a B&Q store? Johnson – who was 'only' on £30,000 a year – apparently said he wasn't feeling very flush.

 When the toilet seat first went missing, B&Q informed the police, but they said they had nothing to go on. Sorry for that one, Saint . . . borrowed from the Two Ronnies, circa 1975.

I used to be a bit of a tennis nut back in the sixties and seventies, and had a court in my garden. As a left-hander, I liked to watch the lefties. Rod Laver was the king of them all, but Jimmy Connors and John McEnroe were more entertaining to watch.

In one of McEnroe's last appearances in a Grand Slam – it was the French Open in Paris – they were experimenting with the Cyclops electronic line-judge system. After a close call went against him, McEnroe got on his hands and knees in front of the machine, studied it for a while and then said: 'I'm not being paranoid, but I swear he knows who I am!'

Mac, in his Superbrat days before morphing into one of the greatest of all commentators, was the king of the insults. I heard him shouting at a linesman during a tele-vised match: 'You can't see as well as the f***** flowers – and they're f***** plastic!'

John McEnroe, these days a court jester (AP Photo/Marcio Jose Sanchez).

In our playing days, Saint, if you said 'boo' to a ref or linesman you were in the book.

 David Beckham, of all people, put his tongue to one of the worst insults, and got red-carded for it. This was in his Real Madrid days. He had been learning to speak Spanish, and unwisely elected to try it out by saying to the referee: '*Hijo de puta*.' This translates as 'son of a whore'. Becks explained that he'd heard other players using the expression and didn't realise just how insulting it was.

 An even bigger insult, Saint, was when Becks described the Spice Girls as the world's greatest singing group. I heard that he was considering singing with them, and they were trying to think of a suitable name, along the lines of Posh Spice, Scary Spice and Sporty Spice. Best they could come up with was Waste of Spice.

 But Beckham has the last laugh on us, Greavsie. He earns more in a year than you and I together picked up in our entire careers.

 True, Saint. And think how much more he'd earn if he could kick with BOTH feet.

Saint's Sports Joke

A child custody case was being held in a West London court. The judge was not sure which of the parents was fit to be granted full custody, so he decided to ask the little boy's view.

'Would you like to live with your mother?' he asked.

'No,' said the boy firmly.

'Why not?' asked the judge.

'Because she beats me.'

The judge said: 'In that case you can go and live with your father.'

'Oh no!' the boy cried. 'He beats me too.'

Exasperated, the judge said: 'Okay, who do you want to live with?'

'I want to live with Fulham,' the boy said.

'Why Fulham?' asked the judge.

'They never beat anybody.'

Greavsie's Sports Joke

Ji-Sung Park, Man United's South Korean midfielder, is at Manchester Airport waiting for a flight home at the end of the season. He decides to go to the currency exchange desk to change his pounds into the more flexible currency of US dollars.

He hands over £100 and gets the equivalent in dollars. As he counts his money, he feels he has been short-changed.

'Wait a minute,' he says to the assistant behind the counter. 'When I came here last month I got more dollars for my pound. What's going on here?'

'Fluctuations,' says the Mancunian clerk.

Ji-Sung gets really mad and replies, 'Well, fluck you English, too!'

The Talk of Sport

Murray Walker

You watch the pit lane while I stop the start watch . . .

Ron Atkinson

I never criticise referees and I'm not going to change a habit for that prat.

Chris Waddle

Peter Crouch is starting to look a bit leggy up front.

Robbie Keane

The penalty – I have to choose my words very carefully . . . it was a disgrace.

David Beckham

My parents have been there for me ever since I was about seven.

Neville Southall

If you don't believe you can win, there is no point in getting out of bed at the end of the day.

Bob Norster, Cardiff Blues chief executive, announcing the arrival of a legend:

Just so you know, we are signing Jonah Lomu and NOT Joanna Lumley.

Rio Ferdinand

Gary Neville is the club captain but has been injured for the best part of a year now, so Giggsy's taken on the mantelpiece.

Graeme Souness

Matt Le Tissier was a super striker of the ball, but he never played for a big club. If he had, we'd be talking about him as a super striker of the ball.

Chris Coleman

Our destiny is in our own hands. We've got six games left – two at home and three away.

Alex Higgins

It's perfectly true. I swear it on my late mother's life.

Keith Hill, Rochdale manager reflecting on a home defeat:

You can compare us at the moment to a bit of soft porn – there's an awful lot of foreplay and not a lot going on in the box.

2 RUN FOR YOUR MONEY

 Right, Greavsie, we've talked a load of balls. Now what about sports played without a ball. How d'you feel, for instance, about athletics?

 Not my scene, Saint. I could never see the sense of running without a ball at my feet. You're talking to the man who once got fined by Spurs for hitching a lift on a milk float during a pre-season cross-country run. As for running marathons, that is definitely a no-go area. Nearest I ever got to a Marathon was eating one. How about you? Were you ever into athletics?

 I loved athletics when I was a wee lad. I belonged to Motherwell Harriers Athletics Club, and was so proud to wear my club vest. My speciality event was the hurdles, and I used to daydream of competing in the Olympics. Then football took over, but I never lost my urge to run and to be as fit as possible.

Fitness was always an important part of my game, and this played a big part in one of the most memorable moments of my career. I headed Liverpool's winning goal in the 1965 FA

Cup final against Leeds, with the game into extra-time and many of the other players going down with cramp and completely exhausted.

It was round about that time that a Liverpool fan famously scrawled one of the great football lines on a church poster near Anfield. Alongside the question 'What Will You Do When Jesus Comes Back?' he wrote: 'Move St John to inside-left.'

 I got quite interested in athletics in the days when Seb Coe, Steve Ovett and Steve Cram were dominating the metric mile, but I've gone off the sport since so many drug cheats have been exposed.

I feel sorry for the athletes who are clean. Most medal-winners are immediately distrusted because of all those who have been caught. Look at the Marion Jones case. I thought I was watching the greatest woman sprinter of all time, and now discover her extra speed came from the science laboratory.

Tell you what, Saint, she'll take some catching if she breaks out of prison.

 I was at an awards ceremony back in the 1960s after Lynn Davies had won the men's long jump gold medal for Britain at the Tokyo Olympics. He won an award but couldn't get along to collect it. The chairman of the sponsors announcing the awards told a celebrity-packed audience at the posh Park Lane hotel: 'Lynn Davies unfortunately can't be with us, but we send her our love wherever she is!'

Terry Downes, then the world middleweight champion, was sitting at my table, and shouted out: 'Give her a kiss from me.'

 The great Miruts 'The Shifter' Yifter was one of the favourites for the 5000 metres in the 1972 Munich

Lynn 'The Leap' Davies, who jumped to Olympic gold in Tokyo in 1964 (Topham Picturepoint/PA Photos).

Olympics, but when the runners lined up at the start he was nowhere to be seen. Miruts was later found in tears at the trackside. He explained that when the athletes had been called up to their mark he was locked in the toilet. Four years later he missed the Montreal Games because of the African boycott, but got his long overdue glory in Moscow in 1980 when he won both the 5000 and 10,000 metres. He was quite flushed with his success!

 Seb Coe, as you know, Greavsie, is an avid Chelsea fan. One day he arrived late for a match at Stamford Bridge and on the wrong side of the stadium. He told the gateman that he would like to get into the ground and make his way through to the main stand. 'Can't let you in this side with that ticket, mate,' said the Jobsworth. 'But I'm Sebastian Coe,' pleaded Seb. 'In that case,' said Jobsworth, 'it will only take you a minute to run to the right entrance.'

 Good joke, Saint, but a *true* story about Seb was when he was warming up for his first major challenge in a British international vest. It was the European Indoor Championships at San Sebastian in 1977. All around him coaches were shouting advice and instructions to their charges. Seb had always been used to the detailed instructions of his father and coach, Peter. He waited and wondered what British team manager Brian Stinson would find to say to him in the moments before his vital 800 metres race. When the runners were called to the arena, Stinson walked over to Coe and said simply, 'Well, bye-bye then.'

Coe won the title in a tenth of a second outside the world record!

 A miler who could be mentioned in the same breath as Seb Coe is New Zealander Peter Snell, who dominated the track in the early 1960s. The world was amazed to hear that he had almost been tripped up by a rabbit while breaking the world half-mile record on a grass track in Christchurch in 1962. Then a correction came over the news agency wires. He had side-stepped a hare (a pacemaker) on his way to the record!

 The story I'm about to tell, Saint, will take some believing and is probably the weirdest in our collection, but it's perfectly true.

Back in the 1930s, Helen Stephens and – here's a mouthful – Stanislawa Walasiewicz monopolised women's sprinting. Miss W, competing for her native Poland but raised in the United States, was Olympic 100 metres champion in 1932, and took the silver behind Miss Stephens in the 1936 Berlin Olympics.

Polish officials accused Miss Stephens of being more man than woman, and she took a sex test to disprove the allegation.

She retired with an unbeaten sprint record, while her arch rival Miss Walasiewicz – who changed her name to Stella Walsh – continued her career, during which she set eleven world records and won forty-one USA sprint championships.

On 4 December 1980 – forty years after hanging up her spikes – Miss Walsh was out shopping at a Cleveland, Ohio, store when innocently caught in the crossfire during a robbery attempt. She was shot dead.

An autopsy revealed that the athletics heroine of the 1930s had male sexual organs. The Polish officials had levelled their accusations at the wrong athlete.

 Och, Greavsie, there has to be question marks about dozens of those Eastern European athletes who dominated the women's Olympic medals back in the Cold War days. Many of them had thicker moustaches than you.

 There was the famous case of Dora Ratjen, who competed for Germany in the 1936 Berlin Games, finishing fourth in the women's high jump. Twenty years later Dora confessed she was in fact Hermann, and that he had been forced by the Nazi Youth Movement to disguise himself as a woman to compete in the Games. He strapped his family jewels to his thigh, which is enough to make any man jump sky high.

 How about the case of Ewa Klobukowska, who won two sprint medals for Poland at the 1964 Tokyo Olympics, but was later banned from athletics after failing a gender test. She was medically judged to be more he than she. Three years later she married and gave birth to a son, which confused everybody.

 I suppose if she'd competed in the AAA championships she'd have run for Middlesex. Remember the Russian Press sisters, Tamara and Irina? They dominated women's athletics in the 1960s, Tamara in the shot put and discus, and Irina in the pentathlon and hurdles. Both were built like brick outhouses, and it was claimed they were hermaphrodites. When gender tests were introduced, surprise, surprise they both announced their retirements. They had muscles in places where most women don't even have places.

 Well, there was no question that Eric Liddell was all man. There have been few greater Scottish sporting heroes. The Reverend Liddell was Britain's champion and record holder over 100 yards, but he declined to take part in the Olympic 100 metres in the 1924 Paris Games because the heats were run on a Sunday.

The never-on-Sunday sprinter, also a Scottish rugby international, decided instead to compete in the 200 metres – in which he took the bronze medal – and the 400, an event in which he was a comparative novice.

Drawn in the outside lane in the final, he hurtled away at the gun and left the American favourites floundering as he rushed to a world record and a golden victory. Liddell, who later became a missionary in China, had his friendly rivalry with 100 metres gold medallist Harold Abrahams captured in the Oscar-winning film *Chariots of Fire*.

 I remember watching the 1968 Olympics on the box when David Hemery won the 400 metres hurdles in a new world record. Commentator David Coleman got so carried away that he screamed into the microphone, 'Who cares who's third . . .' At that precise moment Britain's John Sherwood was literally throwing himself across the line to snatch the bronze medal. Coleman had to apologise.

 John's wife, Sheila, took the silver in the long jump at the same Games. Their son, David, played Davis Cup tennis and John's brother, Steve, was a good-class goalkeeper with Chelsea and then Watford. They had a full Sherwood forest of talent.

Let's move away from athletics now, Greavsie, and talk about other non-ball sports. D'you follow the horses?

 Only to collect dung for my roses, 'cos as you know, Saint, I'm a bit of a gardening fanatic. I've always loved to watch horse racing, but have never been a mug punter. My old Tottenham team-mate Bobby Smith was the king punter, and he was always gambling away his win bonuses on the gee-gees. Manager Bill Nicholson once called us to a team meeting in Amsterdam during a European Cup campaign to rollock us for sending the hotel telephone bill sky high. Smithy had to own up that he was the culprit. He had been phoning bets to his bookmaker.

 I think Stan Bowles would have given Smithy a run for his money as to which footballer was the biggest gambler. I always remember Joe Mercer once saying – when he was manager at Manchester City – that if Stan could have passed a betting shop like he passed a ball he would have been a much more successful player.

We're in dangerous territory here, Saint. There are dozens of footballers that could claim the king of the gamblers crown. I don't think many could beat the heavy Arsenal mob of Kenny Sansom, Paul Merson and Ray Parlour. But everything's relative. It became public knowledge that Wayne Rooney, for instance, had run up seven hundred grand in betting debts, but for him that's a little more than a month's wages. In our day, footballers would often run up bills of five grand, which was close to a year's salary.

Talking of Ray Parlour, it was Ray who came up with one of the great lines during Glenn Hoddle's reign as England manager. Hoddle insisted that his players receive a visit from Eileen Drewery, the notorious faith healer. Most players were happy to go along with the boss and listen to twenty minutes of what they considered weird preparation for a football match. Not Essex joker Parlour, though. As Ms Drewery closed her eyes, put her hands to his head and asked him what he most wanted, Ray answered, 'a short back and sides'.

When this was reported back to Hoddle, it went down like a lead balloon, and Ray is convinced it cost him a longer run in the England team.

 Aye, and it was Ray who was said to have christened Arsène Wenger 'Inspector Clouseau' when the Frenchman first arrived at Highbury. Before one Arsenal game, Wenger had to excuse himself to go to the toilet just as the players were heading down the tunnel. Just about that moment there was a security alert and the team was sent back to the dressing room.

When Arsène reappeared from the loo, he was surprised to find the players hanging about, and asked what was going on.

Before anyone else could answer, Ray – doing a perfect impression of Peter Sellers as Clouseau – said: 'There is a burm.'

Utterly confused, Wenger replied, as if scripted: 'A burm? You say there is a burm?'

As the team fell about laughing, Parlour managed: 'Yes, a burm', before collapsing along with the other players.

Wenger won himself a lot of points from the players by taking it well, saying to Parlour: 'Raymond, I do believe you are having a joke with me.'

 I have owned various bits and pieces of syndicate racehorses over the years, a hoof, a fetlock, a nostril but never an entire horse. But I was never mug enough to put too much money on them.

You have to go back all the way to 1863 for the best Epsom Derby story. The famous racing cry 'They're off!' was heard so many times that when the race finally got under way a lot of people didn't believe it. There were no fewer than thirty-four false starts! Many of them were caused by rank outsider Tambour Major, who was finally left behind. George Fordham, one of the all-time great jockeys, was riding the favourite, which was beaten by a neck.

On his way back to the unsaddling enclosure, Fordham – nicknamed 'The Demon' – overheard a spectator say that he had thrown the race. He leapt off his horse, grabbed hold of the punter and hurled him into a bed of prickles.

 Another great story I've found from that period was the Derby of 1846, when the leading jockey coming off Tattenham Corner was as drunk as a skunk. The man in the saddle was William Scott, one of the outstanding jockeys of his time and younger brother of John Scott, the legendary 'Wizard of the North' trainer.

Scott was riding Sir Tatton Sykes, which he also owned. He had ridden it to victory in the 2000 Guineas and it was highly fancied for the Derby. But as Scott stood at the Epsom bar getting steadily sloshed, the odds of his horse drifted until it had gone out to 16-1.

He had to be helped into the saddle, and was so engrossed in a slanging match with the starter that he didn't see the flag fall and was left several lengths behind the field.

Scott stormed after his departing rivals, still shouting abuse over his shoulder at the starter.

Riding flat out, he stormed through the field and was leading by the time they got to Tattenham Corner. But the booze then caught up on Scott, and he started to take a diagonal course towards the stand. Sam Day drove the chestnut Pyrrhus the First through on the rails to win by a neck.

Scott piloted Sir Tatton Sykes to victory in the St Leger three months later, and the sobering fact is that Sir Tatton could have become the first horse to win the Triple Crown.

 There's no disputing that Martin Pipe has been one of the finest racehorse trainers of modern times, but even he couldn't have matched the ingenuity of his wife, Carol, during a meeting at Taunton in 1993. The Pipe stable were running Elite Reg, and just before he was due to go down to the start it was discovered that his tongue strap was missing.

Carol dashed to the ladies', slipped off her tights and these were used to hold down the horse's tongue. Alas, all to no avail. Elite Reg was pulled up during the race. It was suggested that he had found the course too tight.

 Steve Donoghue, one of the most successful jockeys of the twentieth century, was carrying extra weight when he rode

Humorist to victory in the 1921 Derby. While waiting for the 'off', he had been served a writ for an alleged unpaid debt. He calmly tucked the writ into his silks, and proceded to ride one of his greatest races.

 In my view, two of the people who've led the perfect sporting lives are Francis Lee and Mike Channon. Each of them had outstanding football-playing careers before switching to successful new lives as horse racing trainers. Lee, of course, went on to buy Manchester City and to have a string of business interests.

These days managers and players can afford to get involved on a major scale. Michael Owen and Alan Shearer are heavily into owning racehorses, as are Robbie Fowler, Steve McManaman and, of course, Sir Alex Ferguson.

The story goes that a horse visited Old Trafford and asked Sir Alex for a football trial. Astonished that the horse could talk, Fergie let him kick a ball around, and was even more amazed to see him out-dribbling Ronaldo, shooting harder than Rooney and tackling quicker than Ferdinand.

He took the horse on one side and said, 'Okay. Now let's see you run without a ball.'

The horse replies: 'Run? You've gotta be joking. If I could run I'd be at Ascot not Old Trafford.'

 My fellow Scot Willie Carson tells a lovely true story of his days as one of the greatest of all jockeys. He was racing towards the winning post at Pontefract with what he thought was a comfortable lead when he suddenly sensed a challenge coming on his outside. He called for a greater effort from his mount, but still he was aware of a shadow looming on his shoulder. 'I drove my horse even harder and was relieved to get past the post in first place,' said Willie. 'Then I looked behind me to see how close the other horse was. I couldn't see a thing. I'd spent the last couple of furlongs racing my own shadow! The official winning distance was fifteen lengths.'

 There was an amusing story when I was working at Central Television, and Gary Newbon volunteered to read it out. This was how it read, verbatim:

'We have caught wind of a story that has caused quite a stink at the Fartown ground of Rugby League club Huddersfield, where that great character Alex Murphy is the coach. Alex is a member of a syndicate that paid £10,000 for a National Hunt racehorse. They applied to the Jockey Club to have the horse registered under the name of Fartowner – as in Far Towner. The stewards of the Jockey Club have turned up their noses at this, claiming that the name is not suitable. So the syndicate have settled for the name Claret and Gold, Huddersfield's colours. The radio and television horse-racing commentators will be relieved that Fartowner was not accepted. They still have pronunciation problems with a horse glorying in the name of Hoof Hearted!'

 In France, they turned down the registration of a horse called *Gros Nichons* because they considered it too rude. The owners then simply converted it to English and everyone was happy. The translation – Big Tits!

On our side of the Channel, the Jockey Club refused to register horses with names Wear The Fox Hat and Ho Lee Fook.

Did you know, Greavsie, that when Liverpool comedian Freddie Starr bought Minnehoma at Doncaster Sales for 35,000 guineas, he made his bids by sticking his tongue out at the auctioneer! Later, he was able to stick his tongue out at the bookies when it won the 1994 Grand National at odds of 16-1.

 One of my great heroes was Lester Piggott, who always had a huge following from England when he rode at Longchamp. His army of fans, who had come out on charter flights, celebrated heavily when he won the Arc de Triomphe on Alleged in 1977. One of his followers was poured on the flight for the homeward journey, and he was halfway across the Channel when he became sober enough to remember that he had driven out to Paris.

 Lester was always introverted, and Frankie Dettori is the complete opposite. When he won the 2007 Epsom Derby on Authorized at his fifteenth attempt he made his usual flying dismount, and then gave us a typical over-the-top Frankie quote: 'As I entered the final furlong it was if the world had stopped. Then my heart stopped. I had been dreaming of this moment all my life, and suddenly it was coming true. I laughed, and then I cried. This is the happiest moment of my life.' Frankie then said he was speechless, and continued to talk for another fifteen minutes! He provided more than all Lester Piggott's quotes put together after his nine Derby victories!

 Now for a true story about another four-legged animal. Cockney comedian Tommy Trinder was one of football's outstanding personalities when he was chairman of Fulham. He once walked into the dressing room at Craven Cottage to find trainer Frank Penn massaging a greyhound.

'What's that?' asked Tommy. 'Our new centre-forward?'

'It's a greyhound,' said the trainer.

'I can see that,' said Tommy. 'But what's it doing here?'

'It belongs to Charlie Mitten,' explained Frank. 'We're getting it into the mood for tonight's big race.'

Charlie Mitten, Fulham's outside-left who could have been a prototype for Del Boy Trotter, came in at this point.

'There you are, guv'nor,' said Charlie. 'Been looking for you to tell you about the dog.'

Tommy, accustomed to Charlie's ducking and diving, replied: 'Oh, that's most considerate of you to tell me that we've given a bloody greyhound the run of Craven Cottage.'

'Do yourself a favour, guv'nor,' said cheeky Charlie, 'and get your pound notes on it. It's running at Slough tonight and it's a racing certainty to finish first.'

'But you can't train greyhounds here,' protested Tommy. 'This is a football club. Well, that's what I'm led to believe.'

'I think you'll have to turn a blind eye just this once, guv'nor,' said Charlie, famous for his persuasive tongue. 'All the players have got their money on it, and it'll upset them if we upset the dog.'

Tommy knew when he was beaten. He shrugged and handed Charlie a white fiver. 'Here,' he said. 'Put this on for me when you go to the track.'

The dog trailed in last.

How about motorsport, Greavsie? You've been a bit of a driver in your time. I remember you taking part in the 1970 World Cup Rally from London to Mexico City. Wouldn't it have been easier to try to travel with the England team?

Alf Ramsey had made it clear to me by then that I was no longer part of his plans after I'd told him I wasn't interested in joining his squad just for training sessions and then sitting on the bench. You know me and training, Saint. I always found it a bore. So I thought I'd put some excitement into my life by taking part in the World Cup Rally with co-driver Tony Fall, who was a professional and gave me a crash course – not literally, of course – in rally driving. I was still at Tottenham at the time, and I don't think manager Bill Nicholson was best pleased with me spending more time behind the wheel than kicking a ball.

It was about then, Greavsie, that I was getting my first taste of television work as a member of the BBC studio panel for the World Cup in Mexico. We had a huge team, I remember, including Brian Clough, Johnny Haynes, Ray Wilson, Noel Cantwell, Bob Wilson and referee Jim Finney. It was difficult to get a word in, while over on ITV they were revolutionising football punditry with their 'Four Musketeers', Malcolm Allison, Derek Dougan, Paddy Crerand and Bob McNab.

Didn't you win a BBC football commentary competition that year?

I was runner-up to a Welsh schoolteacher called Idwal Robling. We had come through a series of commentating heats, seeing off dozens of other rivals including Clive Tyldesley. It was then left to Alf Ramsey to decide which of the two of us should win the competition. He picked Robling . . . Why are you laughing, Greavsie?

You had no chance, being a Jock. It was well known that Alf hated the Scots. I was alongside him when we arrived at Glasgow Airport for a Home Championship match back in the 1960s, and as we came through customs a Jock

Saint and Clive Tyldesley, taking the mic (Steve Mitchell/PA Photos).

shouted: 'Welcome to Scotland.' Alf replied: 'You must be f****** joking!'

So we had a lot in common even back then. Alf didn't pick either of us when it really mattered! Anyway, tell us how you got on in the World Cup Rally.

It was one of the toughest things I ever did, Saint. How I survived in one piece I'll never know. Only twenty-three of the ninety-six starters from Wembley Stadium finished the 16,245-mile race. Thanks mainly to the brilliant driving of my co-driver Tony Fall, we finished sixth in our Ford Escort that I thought several times during the marathon was going to become our hearse.

We used to go fifty-five hours in one stretch without sleep as we navigated the toughest terrain in the world, driving at speeds of up to 100 mph on roads that were built with only donkey transport in mind. I remember us being 5,000 feet up into the Andes on a narrow, winding mountain road when we lost a rear wheel. We had already used our spare, and we finished that stage with me at the wheel and Tony at the back pushing.

In all we suffered eleven punctures, a damaged suspension and a broken half shaft. But we got our battered vehicle through to the finish in Mexico after witnessing the aftermath of a terrible earthquake in Lima and landslides in Ecuador.

Rather you than me, Greavsie. I once drove for hundreds of miles in South Africa with my family when I played down there towards the end of my career. We just wanted to see as much as we could, and it's only now looking back that I realise just how dangerous it was. I drove without as much as a spare wheel, and was told later that I must have been mad. There were still a lot of tensions down there then, and I have to admit that it was not the wisest thing I ever did. Didn't you arrive in Mexico City just as the Bobby Moore bracelet scandal was breaking?

Yes, Bobby had just flown in from Bogota after his infamous arrest on a trumped-up jewel theft charge. He had been hidden away on the outskirts of Mexico City in a British embassy house. As you know, Mooro was my best pal and I told the press he would not take a liberty let alone a bracelet.

The press were camped outside the house where he was staying, but they were not letting anybody in. I shinned over the garden wall and was just about to knock on the French windows when the embassy official's wife saw me and gave me a verbal volley. I had to go back over the wall,

Greavsie with his best friend and old drinking buddy Bobby Moore (S&G/PA Photos).

and then ring the front doorbell. It just happened her husband was a Spurs fan, and when he knew it was me he shouted for his wife to let me in. She nearly fainted when my first words to Bobby were: 'Let's have a look at the bracelet, Mooro.'

We raided the embassy cocktail cabinet and had a good drinking session. Mooro and I were just practising for the many long sessions we were to have together when I joined him at West Ham that following season.

 There are a lot of non-ball sports in which the pros don't have to run for their money – although they're each pretty speedy in one way or another. They include swimming, cycling, rowing, skiing, skating and, a load of bull, archery.

 Why don't we chuck in darts, as well? I could throw a nifty arrow, and once played a game on television with the

Crafty Cockney, Eric Bristow. It was round about the time he was developing 'dartitis', the equivalent of golf's yips. He told me he was struggling to let the dart leave his hand, but he still thrashed me.

Here's one for the 'Not a lot of people know that' trivia collectors. Eric told me that he is a polydactyl, with six toes on his right foot. He reckoned it helped him with his balance.

 Bristow was a great character, but even he would have to bow the knee to Jocky Wilson as the most eccentric of the world champions. Jocky never ever cleaned his teeth, claiming his gran had told him 'the English poison the water'. He did not have a tooth in his head by the time he was twenty-eight.

Following his 1982 World final victory over Bristow, he was

Jocky Wilson, the Toothless Tiger of the oche (PA Photos).

persuaded to buy a full set of dentures for £1200, but he never took to them. He gave up wearing the false teeth after they'd flown out of his mouth while he was on the oche in a competition. He later used them as a ball marker while playing pool with Bristow.

The Crafty Cockney and the Mad Jock. They don't make them like that any more, Saint.

And talking of characters, how about British yachtsmen Alan Warren and David Hunt, who were noted for their zany and sometimes eccentric humour? They went overboard with their jokes during the 1976 Olympics, and got warned for their behaviour after they had posed as naval officers working on behalf of the Queen. They 'screened' the Canadian police who had been appointed as Her Majesty's bodyguards.

The two jokers saved their biggest laugh for the actual competition. They were so disillusioned after their Tempest class yacht, *Gift 'Orse*, had broken down for a third time that they set light to it, and sat in a dinghy watching it burn until a coastguard rammed it and sent it to the bottom of Lake Ontario. Hunt, crewman to Warren, told astonished press reporters: 'My skipper is lacking in style. I told him his place as the captain was with the ship, but – shamefully – he refused to go down with it.'

They were the same Games in which the man who became known as the Phantom Fencer got caught. Boris Onischenko, an army major from the Ukraine and competing for the Soviet Union, was one of the world's leading modern pentathletes and was particularly successful in the fencing discipline.

His British opponent in the 1976 Games was Adrian Parker, who was convinced he had not been hit by Onischenko, yet his automatic light register lit up. Parker's team-mate, Jeremy Fox, had the same experience and the jury were asked to examine the Russian's épée.

It was discovered that it had been wired with a hidden push-button circuit breaker, which enabled Onischenko to register hits at will. He was disqualified and sent back to the Soviet Union in disgrace. He was dubbed 'Disonischenko'.

 The Russians would go to any lengths to win medals. There was an extraordinary story during the 1980 Games in Moscow. It was alleged that every time Soviet throwers were preparing to run up during the men's javelin event, the huge stadium doors behind them would be opened, causing a draft that gave them the advantage of a following wind. The doors, it was claimed, remained closed while non-Soviet athletes took their throws. Russian throwers came first and second, and a lot of competitors reckoned their chances had gone with the wind.

 One Soviet sportsman who did not need to cheat was the great Vyacheslav Ivanov, who even today is recognised as one of the greatest ever scullers. The man from Moscow won gold medals in the single sculls in 1956, 1960 and 1964. He was so excited when he won his first gold in Melbourne in 1956 that he tossed his medal high in the air in delight. As he reached out to catch his prized possession he succeeded only in knocking it into the lake. The eighteen-year-old Ivanov dived into the water along with several rival rowers, but they could not retrieve it. The International Olympic Committee later presented him with a replacement medal.

No question about the prize for the funniest rowing moment. It goes to that lovely old BBC commentator Harry Carpenter, who told viewers at the end of the Boat Race: 'Ah, isn't that nice. The wife of the Cambridge President is kissing the cox of the Oxford crew.'

Saint's Darts Jokes

A group of nuns called in for refreshing glasses of lemonade while a darts match was taking place in a Liverpool pub. They took a close interest in the darts, and one of them – very short-sighted – got as near as she could to the board. One of the darts players threw two successive double tops, and then his third dart hit the rim and bounced back. It struck the short-sighted nun in the middle of the forehead, killing her instantly. The marker called out: 'One nun dead and eighty.'

* * *

Practising for a pub darts tournament, Pete decided to experiment by using the spinning action of a hammer thrower. He lost control of the dart and it hit the barman between the eyes.

As the barman collapsed to the floor, quick-thinking Pete used his mobile to phone for an ambulance.

He told the emergency operator: 'Help, I think I may have accidentally killed a barman! What do I do?'

The operator, used to panic calls, said with a reassuring voice, 'First of all go to him and make sure he's really dead.'

Listening on the phone, the operator was startled to hear a thumping noise, followed by muffled moaning and then silence.

A few seconds later, Pete was back on the line telling her: 'Okay, now what do I do?'

Greavsie's
Horse Racing Jokes

A distressed wife took her husband to the doctor and said: 'Please help us. My husband thinks he's a horse.'

'How long has this been going on?' asked the doctor.

'Several months,' the wife said. 'He insists on only eating oats, and I have turned our garage into a stable so that he can sleep on a straw bed.'

'Well, I will have to admit him to hospital for treatment,' the doctor said. 'I think he should come in immediately.'

'Thank you, doctor,' the wife said. 'But can you leave his admission until the weekend. He's running in the two-thirty at Newmarket tomorrow.'

* * *

While riding the favourite at the Boxing Day meeting at Kempton, the jockey was suddenly clonked on the head by a stuffed turkey and a volley of walnuts. He managed to control the horse before clearing the next fence and regaining the lead.

As he approached the last fence he was hit by a box of Christmas crackers and a dozen mince pies, and in the final furlong was overtaken as he dodged a bottle of sherry and a Christmas pudding.

The owner immediately lodged an objection with the stewards because his horse had been hampered.

The Talk of Sport

George Orwell

Serious sport is war minus the shooting.

Greg LeMond

You don't suffer, kill yourself and take the risks I take just for money. I love bike racing.

Ted Walsh, racing commentator

This is really a lovely horse and I speak from personal experience since I once mounted her mother.

Woody Allen

I was not into sports, although one year I tried hard to get into the chess team. I failed to make it because of my height.

Yogi Berra, baseball great

Half the lies they tell about me aren't true.

George Foreman

I guessed it was time for me to hang up my gloves when I was shadow boxing, and the shadow whupped me.

Ron Pickering

And there goes Juantorena down the back straight, opening his legs and showing his class.

Anita Lonsbrough

It's obvious the Russian swimmers are determined to do well on American soil.

Dave Brenner

If our swimmers want to win any medals they had better get their skates on.

Mario Andretti

If everything seems under control when you're driving an F1 car you're just not going fast enough.

Daley Thompson

Being a decathlete is like having ten girlfriends. You have to love them all, and you can't risk falling out with any of them.

Steve Ovett

The decathlon is nine Mickey Mouse events and the 1500 metres.

David Bean

Cycling is a good thing for the youngsters, because it keeps them off the streets.

Lester Piggott

Never catch a loose horse. You could end up holding the f****** thing all day.

Larry Hagman

I like racehorses but will never own one. I don't like anything that eats while I sleep.

Clement Freud

Owning a racehorse is probably the most expensive way of gaining entry to a racecourse for nothing.

3 IT'S A KNOCKOUT

 Let's talk boxing, Greavsie. I know you're bursting to tell about the day you got into the ring with Mike Tyson.

 It was one of my most memorable television interviews for our *Saint and Greavsie* show. At the time Tyson was being billed as the 'Baddest Man on the Planet'. I met him in his training camp tucked away in the Catskill Mountains in New York, where he was preparing for his world title defence against Michael Spinks in Atlantic City.

He trained in a small gymnasium above the cop shop in what was a one-horse town. As I watched him belting sparring partners around the ring as if they were punch bags, I got the feeling that I would not want to tango with Tyson, let alone tangle with him.

I honestly felt I was in the presence of a being from another planet. The first thing that struck me about him was his cliff wall of a body, and in particular a neck that looked as if it might once have been a smoke stack on a tug. But it was not just his physical appearance that was so impressive and also intimidating. He had an aura about him that was almost electric, or even nuclear.

Back in the mid-60s I had met Muhammad Ali when he was in London training for his second fight with Henry Cooper. He too had an aura, but it was one that brought a smile to your face. Tyson brought a chill to the heart. With Ali you felt you were in the company of a great entertainer as much as a great sportsman. With Tyson, the feeling was more of being close to an unexploded bomb.

 This is fascinating stuff, Greavsie, but remember the purpose of the book is to make our readers smile.

 Hold your horses, Saint. I'll get to the funny bit eventually. But let me set the scene first. I climbed into the ring to chat with Tyson in front of the television cameras. He gave me a riveting fifteen-minute interview during which he playfully patted me in the ribs, and left a small bruise that I wore like a badge of honour. Mike sounded like a surgeon about to perform a cutting operation as he showed me how he went about mounting a body attack.

'The main target areas,' he said as he pushed me into a corner of the ring under a mock (thank God) assault, 'are the liver, the kidney region, the heart, the floating rib and the abdomen.'

I naively said that I thought kidney punches were illegal, and he laughed like a drain. 'Hey, man, we're not talking Marquess of Queensbury rules here,' he said. 'I'm defending the world heavyweight championship, the greatest prize in sport. If you can get on the referee's blind side and land a punch to the kidneys, that's all part and parcel of the fight game.'

I remember when you and our director Ted Ayling got back from the interview. The pair of you talked about it as if you'd been on a safari rather than to cover a sports story.

That's a perfect description, Saint. It was like being in the company of an animal. He brought his massive right fist up into my soft underbelly. 'Then there's the solar plexus punch,' he said. 'It was invented by that great English fighter of yours, Bob Fitzsimmons, when he knocked out James J. Corbett to become the world heavyweight champion. It was a remarkable performance by Fitz because he weighed no more than a middleweight.'

All these body bits, Greavsie, and he's not mentioned the ears? I thought he was partial to them.

The ear-biting with Evander Holyfield came much later in his career. He was not a hungry fighter at this point.

Tyson peppered his conversation on-camera and off with boxing facts. He's a genuine fan of his sport, and a walking record book on its history. I've never spoken to anybody quite like him. He is an uneducated man from the dead end of Brooklyn, yet talked to me like somebody who has swallowed a dictionary. He wouldn't win any prizes in the academic world, but has a street sense of *Mastermind* proportions.

You still haven't got to the funny bit, and he wasn't street smart enough to hang on to his money. He lost millions of dollars.

Smart observation, Saint. I'll come to that side of things in a minute. Mike and I had a long off-camera chat as he was changing in the locker room. One thing I can reveal is that the most impressive part of his anatomy was never seen in public. I'll leave it to your imagination. Let's just say he could have swept the gymnasium floor without a broom! Yet he had a surprisingly high, almost effeminate voice and a slight lisp.

I asked him what it was like to land a knockout punch, and he replied: 'Better than the greatest orgasm you could ever have.'

He told me he'd never forgotten that he'd come from the streets. 'I go back to my old neighbourhood a lot,' he said. 'It does me good to remind myself where my roots are. Man, they are the toughest streets on God's earth. Everybody has to fight just to survive. I go to prisons and drug rehabilitation centres just to give people hope. It makes you want to cry to see old friends who failed to beat the trap into which they were born.'

 Well, he later got to know the inside of prison for real. He got put away for rape, which pretty much destroyed his image and made commentators reach for the old saying that you can take the man out of the ghetto, but you can't take the ghetto out of the man.

 Yes, Saint, but remember when I interviewed him he was being touted as the greatest heavyweight champion of all time, and was on the sane side of the tracks. Tyson told me, and I wrote an article about it for the *Sun* on my return, that he feared falling back into his bad old ways. He told me he was running wild with the street gangs from before he was ten, had been arrested thirty-eight times by the time he was thirteen, and said he had the feeling he was going to end up either going to prison or dead in the gutter.

He was right about going to prison.

 Tyson told me, 'I was reckless and just didn't care one way or another about anything or anyone. It would be easy to be critical of me, but you had to be down there at the bottom to know why I was like it. Then I got lucky and discovered boxing and some good people who believed in me. Now when I go back to my old hang-outs I tell the kids I see on the street corners: "Hey, look what happened for me. You can get out, too, if you just work hard enough and believe in yourself."'

 Well, he let down all those young people who hero-worshipped him. And, Greavsie, you've not made me crack a smile yet.

 Okay, you said about all the millions of dollars that he got through. Well, I got just a taste of his lifestyle when three brand-new Cadillacs were driven up to the gym, each a different colour. Mike came and sat behind the wheel of each one, and just couldn't make up his mind which one he liked best. So he ordered all three! That was just a hint that he was not going to hang on to his millions for long.

 And that's the funny bit?

 The funny story came later from one of Tyson's entourage, who worked the corner as the man in charge of the ice bucket. During one fight they somehow forgot to take the icebag to the ring. This rarely mattered early in his career, because he battered his opponents into quick submission. The night they forgot the icebag Mike got a swelling under an eye. Panic! But the problem was solved when one of the quick-thinking cornermen took a condom out of his wallet, which he filled with iced water and then placed it under Tyson's eye. Somebody said – but not to his face – that it made him look a real dickhead.

I was envious of you, Greavsie, getting to interview Tyson. Boxing was one of my favourite sports when I was growing up in Motherwell. I had a good boxing record at youth level, and remember once being presented with a sugar bowl for winning a tournament. For me, it was as big a thing as winning the Super Bowl.

We had an outstanding local boxer called Chic Calderwood, who became the first Scot to win the British and Commonwealth light-heavyweight titles and he beat top American Willie Pastrano. I wanted to follow in Chic's path, but football got a hold on me and so I hung up my gloves.

Of course, when I got to Liverpool I found Shanks loved his boxing almost as much as football. His idol was Jack Dempsey – 'the greatest fighter ever to pull on a pair of gloves,' he would say. When he was a player at Preston he used to spend a lot of time in the gymnasium hitting a punchbag and shadow boxing in front of the full-length mirror.

I remember Shanks once talking boxing to us in the dressing room before a match for fifteen minutes. Then, with the referee calling us out for the game, he said: 'I didn't want to talk football today because you'll find it easy to beat this lot, provided you keep your guard up and go out fighting.' It was if he was sending us out from the corner for the first round of a fight.

Another time, he walked into the hospitality room at Anfield with half the team, persuading them to join him to watch a fight that was being screened live on television. There were two elderly ladies in the room watching the box. 'Now you wouldn't mind us turning over to the other side to watch the boxing, would you, ladies,' he said, giving a warm smile. He could be quite charming when necessary. One of the ladies said they would like to see the end of the programme they were watching, and Bill said: 'I quite understand, but as we live in a democracy I'm going to put it to the vote. Those who want to watch the boxing, raise your hands . . .!'

Incidentally, it was Willie Pastrano who was fighting in New York once and on the end of a real hiding. He went down for a count of eight, and as he got up the referee, checking his senses, asked: 'What's your name and where are you?'

Willie said through battered lips: 'I'm Willie Pastrano, and I'm in Madison Square Garden getting the shit knocked outta me.'

 I seem to remember you made a boxing comeback against Pancho Pearson at Fulham, Saint.

 Och, he asked for it. He pulled my hair and I instinctively turned and laid him out with a right to the jaw. Shanks made history at the disciplinary hearing by becoming the first manager to present film evidence in defence of a player. He showed TV film in which it was obvious that Pearson was tugging my hair as if he was trying to see if I had a wig on. It didn't help, though. I still got a fine and a suspension.

Even worse was in a Boxing Day match at Coventry in 1967. At a free-kick, Coventry player Brian Lewis did to me what many years later Vinnie Jones would do to Paul Gascoigne. He reached behind and squeezed my testicles very hard. I reacted by chinning him and was sent off instantly.

As I walked towards the dressing room, Shanks came to my side and asked: 'What the hell went on there, son?'

'He grabbed my goolies, Boss.'

'We'll take action, don't you worry,' said Shanks. 'Report early at the ground tomorrow.'

When I got to Anfield the next morning, Shanks and Bob Paisley were waiting for me, and they took me straight into the treatment room. They told me to strip and lie on the treatment table. As I lay on my back, Bob started to dab a piece of cloth soaked in a mix of iodine and boot polish. He spread it on my groin and genitals.

'That'll do, Bob,' said Shanks, inspecting my privates as if he were a doctor.

Shanks then went out of the room and returned moments later with a posse of pressmen that he'd invited to the ground.

'Come and look at this outrage,' Shanks told them. 'Can you wonder why the lad took the action he did? Who wouldn't lash out if that sort of punishment was handed out to them, and I do mean handed out.'

The press boys dashed off and filed stories about the shocking attack on my family jewels. Again, no use. A fine and a three-match suspension.

 Sounds a load of balls to me, Saint.

I played in the match in which my Tottenham teammate Terry Venables and Fulham defender Fred Callaghan famously got sent off for fighting at White Hart Lane. It was a few days after Muhammad Ali had defended his world title with a points victory over Ernie Terrell. During a viciously one-sided contest, Ali – who had just recently changed his name from Cassius Clay – kept baiting the outclassed Terrell by saying: 'What's mah name?'

As Venners and Fred Callaghan – who had grown up together in the same Dagenham streets as me – stood sparring with each other, a voice from the terraces pleaded: 'For Gawd's sake, Tel, tell him yer name . . .!' The referee didn't see the joke, and sent them both off.

There was a game at Charlton when team-mates Derek Hales and Mike Flanagan were sent off for fighting each other, and Graeme Le Saux famously punched David Batty in the face when they were playing for Blackburn in a Champions League game in Moscow.

More recently, of course, Newcastle team-mates Lee Bowyer and Kieron Dyer got their marching orders for having a punch-up while playing at St James' Park. Did you ever whack anybody in a game, Greavsie?

I couldn't punch my way out of a paperbag, Saint, but I once got a ticking-off from the ref for dancing on the pitch. I was playing for Spurs at West Ham, and got hold of my best mate Bobby Moore's arm in the penalty area and we danced around in a circle. While we were dancing I said to Mooro, 'See you in the Black Lion later.'

Bobby was a boxing fanatic, and used to watch all those satellite fights at the cinema that used to take place in the middle of the night. It suited Mooro because he was an insomniac.

He was at the Wembley Arena ringside the night in 1971 when Jerry Quarry, former world heavyweight title challenger, knocked out chicken farmer Jack Bodell in just sixty-four seconds. In the dressing room after his demolition job, Quarry told reporters: 'I knew nothing about Bodell apart from I'd been told he was big and awkward. This proved accurate information. He *was* very big and he fell very awkwardly.'

Shanks used to collect off beat boxing stories, and would pass them on to us during train and coach trips to away matches. One I remember is about former world heavyweight champion Max Baer, who returned to his corner at the end of a round in a title eliminator to be told by his second: 'You're doing great, he ain't laid a glove on ya yet.' Baer replied, 'Well keep an eye on the referee, 'cos somebody's beating the hell outta me.'

It was Baer who said to Primo Carnera as they both tumbled to the canvas during a world title fight: 'Last one up's a cissy.'

 I think the joke would have been wasted on Primo. When he first arrived in the United States from Italy he could just about speak but hardly understand English. Asked at a press conference what he thought of Los Angeles, he said: 'I'll knock da bum out in two.'

 Frank Bruno used to be a regular visitor to our studio. He'd just been beaten by Bonecrusher Smith, and you asked him who he'd like to meet next, and he replied: 'The b****** who matched me with Bonecrusher!'

 I had one of the first on-screen interviews with Frank when he was just starting out as a professional. I drove him up to Birmingham in a powerful Mercedes saloon owned by his manager, Terry Lawless. On the way up I explained to Frank that I wanted to interview him in the ring, both of us with gloves on. We met the Central Television crew at a local gymnasium and got stripped for action.

The sparring session would have made a great sketch for a comedy show. Frank is six inches taller than me, and I was having trouble getting past his long arms to ask my questions.

In those early days in his career muscular Frank was weighing about fifteen stone, and I had ballooned up from my playing days weight of ten stone seven pounds to around thirteen stone. I was a welterweight masquerading

Frank Bruno gets the royal handshake as Sir Jimmy Savile introduces him to Prince Charles (John Stillwell/PA Photos).

in the out-of-condition body of a cruiserweight. Director Syd Kilby's plan was that I should 'fight' my way inside Frank's reach and put a question to him each time I got to close quarters. Syd didn't realise the effort and energy you use just when sparring, particularly against a giant like Bruno. Each time I fought my way close enough to ask a question I was breathing like a wounded bull.

I would start the interview and then the soundman would interrupt and say: 'All I can hear is Greavsie's heavy breathing.'

I said between gasps for air: 'You could sell the sound-track for a bleedin' blue movie.'

After about six tries, it was left to me to change the

plans of the director. I told Syd to forget about the sparring, and I said to Bruno: 'Tell you what, Frank, you rest against the ropes in the corner and I'll interview you there.'

A pity the cameras didn't follow us back down the motorway when we left Birmingham. We stopped off at a service station for a bite to eat and we had the place in uproar. I kept going up to the biggest, toughest-looking lorry drivers I could find and challenging them to a fight. Then I'd point at Frank and say: 'I think you should know that I'm bringing on a sub.'

The biggest laugh of the day was on me. Frank filled three trays with food, and I was left to pay the bill.

 My favourite part of training for boxing was using the skipping rope. I used to see old black and white film of Sugar Ray Robinson doing magical things with the rope, and I taught myself to skip not only at speed but with sudden changes of rhythm and height.

One day at our local Saturday morning pictures they called for volunteers to go up on stage for a skipping contest. About ten girls joined in . . . and me. I got lots of jeers and whistles from the other boys, but they shut up when I outskipped all the girls and won a prize, which was two free tickets for that night's film show. I gave them to my mother.

 You're a bleedin' saint, Saint.

Going back to Bruno, we had a return session in the ring in the days when I had a regular spot on that cult programme *Tiswas*. I had learned from our first meeting in front of the cameras, and this time I rehearsed the interview with Frank before our sparring session that was going out 'live' to the nation.

I worked it out with Frank that I would ask a question and then lightly hit him with three pulled punches. Bang, bang, bang.

Then Frank would reply and hit me with three light punches. Bang, bang, bang.

We got a nice rhythm going at rehearsal. Question – bang, bang, bang. Answer – bang, bang, bang.

Then we went 'live' with the interview in a ring set up in the studio, and Frank suddenly froze with the sort of camera fright that many – including you and me, Saint – had experienced before him.

I asked my first question and lightly hit Frank with three punches. Bang, bang, bang. He replied, and then lightly landed just two punches. Bang, bang. I replied, and gradually we got some sort of a rhythm going, even though Frank had gone tongue-tied and stiff.

By the time of my fifth question, Frank began to relax, but somehow managed to get out of synchronisation.

I asked my question – bang, bang, bang. Instead of replying as we had planned, Frank landed three punches that were twice as hard as usual and caught me completely unawares. My knees buckled and I fell forward into Frank's arms with my head spinning and water streaming from my eyes.

The studio crew were all folded up laughing off-camera as I somehow managed to get through the interview. For the rest of the questions I got myself into a close-quarters clinch rather than risk taking any more out-of-time punches.

After the interview ended, Frank apologised and said with that booming laugh of his: 'Sorry, Jim. I found it easier to punch than talk, know what I mean . . .'

 Rocky Marciano was one of my heroes when I first got interested in boxing. He remains the only world heavyweight champion to retire without a single defeat on his record – forty-nine fights, forty-nine wins. Perfection. He made a comeback of sorts six months before he was killed in a plane crash.

Rocky was persuaded to face Muhammad Ali in a computer fight in front of the film cameras. Every move and punch was choreographed, and they shot four different endings.

They put a wig on Rocky's balding head, and hid his bulging stomach in a pair of specially tailored shorts. 'Hey, d'ya know somethin'?' Rocky said as they fitted his hairpiece. 'This rug cost more than I got for my first professional fight.'

Marciano died the day before his forty-ninth birthday without knowing the result of the phantom fight. A week later the film was released with the version showing him stopping Ali in the tenth round.

Ali said later: 'I went along with it out of respect to Rocky's memory, but the truth is that at my peak he would not have been able to hit me with a handful of rice.'

Of course, Ali had a quote for every occasion but even he was almost lost for words when he heard the size of the alimony cheque he would have to pay his first wife, Sonja, following their divorce in 1967. 'I'm the only one to beat him,' Sonja was reported as saying. 'He's going to remember that every day for the next ten years while he's making his payments.'

When he got his senses back, Ali said: 'I'm having to pay so much money that they've even named the payments after me – *Ali*mony!'

 Nobody could challenge Ali for one-liners. He told a press conference in Munich that he had spied on his British opponent Richard Dunn shadow-boxing in the gymnasium. He paused and then added, with a comedian's timing: 'The shadow won.'

It was Ali who said that he was so fast that when he switched off his light to go to bed he would be between the sheets before it had gone out.

 He used to give Joe Frazier terrible verbal stick. 'Joe's so ugly,' he'd say, 'that when he cries his tears run backwards rather than go down his face . . . He should donate his face to the Wildlife Fund.'

Ali cleverly used words as a psychological weapon. He told Sonny Liston, then considered the most fearsome fighter in the world: 'You ugly bear, you're slow and old. You ain't no champ, you're a chump.' He chipped away at Liston until Sonny completely ran out of belief in himself.

 Our old ITV colleague Reg Gutteridge once won fifty dollars off Sonny. He bet him that he could stick a knife in his leg without even blinking. Sonny, a born gambler, took the bet, and then watched as Reg stabbed his leg with a knife . . . without blinking. Reggie said that Sonny paid up and then fell over laughing when Reggie rolled up his trouser leg to reveal he had a false leg. He had a leg blown off when he stepped on a mine during the Normandy D-Day landings.

 It was nothing new when Mike Tyson chewed Evander Holyfield's ear during a world title fight. Defending the Olympic middleweight championship he had won in 1920, British boxer Harry Mallin was involved in an extraordinary incident in the 1924 quarter-finals against Frenchman Roger Brousse. In the final round, when seeming to be comfortably ahead on points, Mallin was bitten on the chest by Brousse during a close-quarters clinch.

Mallin attempted to protest to the referee, but because of language difficulties could not make himself understood.

Brousse was awarded a controversial points decision, but following a complaint from a neutral Swedish official who had seen the biting incident, the boxing committee held an inquiry. They studied the tell-tale teeth marks on Mallin's chest, and disqualified Brousse and reversed the decision.

Mallin, a London policeman, went on to retain his title by out-pointing his countryman John Elliott in the final.

British champion from 1919 to 1923, Mallin went through his career of more than 200 amateur contests without a single defeat . . . even by a hungry fighter!

After Tyson had bitten a lump out of Holyfield's ear, America's top wax museum moved his image from the sporting heroes section and placed him in the villains area – alongside Hannibal Lecter!

Pat Desmond, a fighter who had the gift of the gab as well as the gift of the jab, was taking a hammering in an all-Ireland heavyweight championship contest and went down on his knees in his own corner early in the second round. His second shouted, 'Don't get up till nine, Pat . . . don't get up till nine . . .' Still kneeling, Pat shouted back: 'And what time is it now?'

Another true Irish story, told me years ago by Paddy Byrne, who was a matchmaker and manager: 'I took a boxer to Denmark for an eight-round fight. We flew from Belfast to Copenhagen. It was his first flight and it took little more than an hour. I thought my boxer was in good shape, and couldn't understand why he was puffing and blowing after only a couple of rounds. As he flopped down on the stool at the bell ending the third, I asked: "What's wrong with you?" He shrugged his shoulders, and said with a straight face and deadly seriousness: "I must be suffering from jet lag."'

Mickey Duff, in his younger days as a manager before becoming a matchmaker, took three boxers over to Belfast to box. He had requested specifically that all three should be put on early so that they could catch the late-night ferry back to England.

'I was furious when I found out one of my boys would be last on,' Mickey said. 'I was just about to give the promoter a piece of my mind when the boxer told me with great confidence, "Don't worry, Mickey. I'll get it over quickly. We'll catch that ferry."

'True to his word, my boy got it over inside the first thirty seconds. He collapsed as if pole-axed from the first punch thrown by his opponent. As I dived anxiously through the ropes to remove his gumshield while he lay flat on his back, he gave me a big wink and said: "I told you we wouldn't miss the ferry."'

It's what is known as a ferry story.

Terry Lawless, who managed Bruno and four world champions – Jim Watt, Maurice Hope, John H. Stracey and Charlie Magri – passed on a fascinating story about another of his boxers, Kirkland Laing.

Kirk was a wonderfully gifted boxer, who once beat the legendary Roberto Duran. He is considered one of the greatest British fighters never to have won a world title. Sadly, he did not have the discipline to go with his enormous talent. In the words of Terry, he was as mad as a March hare, and lived on a planet of his own.

Once when Terry was in his corner during a fight in Southend, he heard somebody whistling and wondered where it was coming from. He suddenly realised it was

Kirk who was whistling a tune through his gumshield as he waltzed around his outclassed opponent.

When he went back to his corner at the end of the sixth round in an eight-round contest, Terry told Kirk: 'If you carry on whistling and giving this fight less than 100 per cent you won't find me here when you come back at the end of the round.'

Kirk being Kirk, he carried on whistling his happy tune. When the bell ended the round, he found he had no manager left in his corner.

'I had to teach him a lesson,' Terry told me. 'I have a great sense of humour, but the boxing ring is not the place for messing about. His clowning was an insult to the spectators and disrespectful to his opponent.'

But Kirk carried on clowning for much of his eventful career during which he won the British, Commonwealth and European welterweight titles. After his major upset victory against Duran in Detroit he disappeared from sight for a year, frittering away all his money on ladies and booze and – allegedly – drugs. During the year that he went missing, Duran took the fight that could have been Laing's and collected £4 million for fighting Marvin Hagler.

Terry Lawless also managed John H. Stracey, whose world title win over Jose Napoles in Mexico was an even greater performance than Kirkland Laing's victory over Duran. John H. is a Cockney through and through, but these days lives near Liverpool and is a regular on the after-dinner circuit in the North-West. He is a great judge of boxing, but I'm not so sure about his taste in footballers. He reckons, Greavsie, that you are the best of all time!

He tells how he was knocked down by Napoles in the first round, and looked out at the 27,000 Mexicans screaming for his blood. He recalls, 'I thought to myself that there was no way I was going to be made to look a fool in front of all these people. So I picked myself up and went for Napoles. I knocked him down in the third and belted him into the ropes in the sixth to force the Mexican referee to stop it. Napoles was God out there, so you can imagine how reluctant the ref was to stop it. He had to show a lot of bravery to wave the fight over, but it was wise because I had Napoles at my mercy.'

John coached the Kemp brothers for their boxing scenes in the acclaimed film, *The Krays*. 'I lived just around the corner to Ronnie and Reggie when I was growing up,' said John. 'They were local heroes, who looked after their own.'

 My lovely old pal Henry – sorry, Sir Henry – Cooper told me this story. He was at a dinner at a posh London hotel where Sir Alf Ramsey was guest of honour, and the then Prime Minister Harold Wilson was making the tribute speech. Suddenly a mouse ran the length of the top table. Harold was unaware and thought his speech was going down a storm as people started to laugh at the mouse. Henry, sitting at the end of the table, suddenly reached out his famous left hand and caught the mouse by its tail. He handed it to a waiter, who passed it to the chef, who stamped on it! The PM realised why his speech was getting a bigger than expected laugh, and said: 'It's the first time one of my speeches has brought the mouse down!'

Saint's Boxing Jokes

A boxer, his battered and bruised hands swathed in bandages, is in a bar having a drink, and the landlord helps raise the glass to his mouth.

The boxer, known as Goya because he's always on the canvas, says: 'I'm going to have to quit the ring. My hands just can't take any more punishment.'

'You've damaged them punching opponents?' the landlord asks.

The boxer shakes his head sadly. 'No, that's not the reason they're damaged,' he confesses. 'It's the referees . . . they keep treading on them.'

* * *

A British boxer was taking time off from training in Las Vegas for a world title challenge by attending a show where a ventriloquist was topping the bill. Unaware that he was in the audience, the vent said: 'That Brit stops so many shots with his face he should be a soccer goalkeeper.'

The fuming British champion stood up and shouted: 'Bet you've never been in the ring in your life. You're so ugly it looks as if you've been used as a punchbag.'

The ventriloquist gulps and starts to apologise. 'Sorry, you're upset,' he said.

'Butt out of this, you,' warned the boxer. 'I'm not talking to you but that blockhead on your lap.'

Greavsie's Boxing Joke

An old boxer who took several punches too many becomes a tramp, and he does odd jobs to keep himself fed and watered. One day he knocks on the door of a posh townhouse, and when the owner opens the door, he asks: 'Please, sir, is there any odd job I can do in return for a meal?'

The owner, an arrogant, stockbroker type, does a double take, and says: 'Didn't you use to be a boxer? I saw you fight for the British title, and you stank the place out. You were a complete mug.'

The ex-pug bites his tongue, and says: 'If you say so, sir. Now is there anything I can do for a meal. I'm starving.'

The house owner laughs. 'A hungry fighter,' he says. 'Okay, if you go around the back, you'll see a gallon of paint and a clean paintbrush. All you have to do is paint my porch, and I'll give you a good meal.'

So the old boxer goes around the back and a while later he again knocks on the door. The owner says, 'Finished already? Good. Come on in. Sit down. The cook will bring your meal right in.'

The old fighter says, 'Thank you very much, sir. But there's something that I have to correct you on. It's not a Porsche you've got there. It's a BMW.'

The Talk of Boxing

Mike Tyson, before fighting Lennox Lewis:

My main objective is to be professional but to kill him.

Joe Louis, before a title fight against Max Schmeling:

Yeah, I'm scared. I'm scared I might kill him.

Dan Duva, boxing promoter/manager on Mike Tyson's release from jail:

Why would anyone expect him to come out smarter? He went to prison for three years, not Princeton.

Ricky Hatton

First thing I'm going to do after I've won the fight is say hello to two friends who I've shut out of my life for the past ten weeks while I trained the hardest I've ever done. So welcome back Mr Guinness and Mr Dom Perignon.

Sir Henry Cooper

Take it from me, there's more tension in golf than in boxing. Golfers tense over the ball, which is silly when you think about it. After all, it's not as if the ball is going to jump up and belt you on the whiskers, is it!

Jake LaMotta, the Raging Bull:

I fought Sugar Ray Robinson so many times it's a wonder I ain't got sugar diabetes.

Amir Khan, after another easy win:

My warm-up was harder than the fight.

Rocky Graziano, former world middleweight champion (played by Paul Newman in *Somebody Up There Likes Me*):

When I was a kid growing up in New York, we only stole things that began with an 'a' – a fridge, a car, a watch . . .

Tony Zale, former world middleweight champion:

I quit school in the sixth grade because of pneumonia. Not because I had it, but because I couldn't spell it.

Muhammad Ali, to challenger Joe Bugner:

If you even *dream* of beating me, you'd better wake up and apologise.

Joe Bugner

Boxers are nothing more than prawns in this game.

Chris Eubank

My biggest mistake was not being born to parents who were accountants.

Nigel Benn

I'm one of the bravest men ever to climb into the ring. My balls are bigger than a cow's.

Sugar Ray Leonard

We're all blessed with God-given talents. Mine was being able to punch people in the head.

Max Baer, after being knocked out by Joe Louis:

He hit me with eighteen punches while I was falling down. With hand speed like that, he'd make a fortune cleaning windows.

Willie Pep, ex-world featherweight champion on retirement:

I've got it made. I've got a wife and a TV set – and they're both working.

Randall 'Tex' Cobb, heavyweight contender:

I was once knocked out by a Mexican bantamweight – six of my pals were swinging him around by his heels at the time.

4   **A BIT OF LEG-OVER**

 I think many people, Greavsie, will be surprised to know that I'm a cricket lover.

 That's unusual for a Jock. Most Scots think extra cover is an extreme form of birth control.

 Quite funny, but totally inaccurate. Douglas Jardine and Mike Denness were Scots who captained England, and Tony Greig had Scottish parents. I fell in love with the game back in the 1950s when I watched on television as 'those little friends of mine, Ramadhin and Valentine' ran through the English batsmen.

It made me want to become a spin bowler, and I used to spend hours out in the street perfecting off-breaks. Luckily, the next summer, we got an English teacher who came to the school and he was mad on cricket.

We formed a school cricket team, and beat most other schools except when we played the toffs at the private schools. We weren't used to playing on grass, like them. Our wickets were concrete.

I remember you making a great career move by bowling television chief Michael Grade.

 That was when I played for London Weekend Television against the BBC. It was on a beautiful ground at Dulwich. Michael, ex-public schoolboy and then the chairman of the BBC, came striding out to the wicket in his immaculate whites, hooped cap and miming imaginary cuts and hooks. He took his guard, and then made a big stride forward ready to drive my first delivery to the covers. The ball spun wickedly and made a mess of his stumps. It was a Shane Warne–Mike Gatting moment. Michael looked completed baffled as he made his way back to the pavilion, while I was celebrating as if I'd scored a winner in front of the Kop.

 Not very bright of you, Saint. I would have let him hit me all over the field.

I once had a similar experience to Michael Grade. Cricket fanatics Frank Nicklin and Reg Hayter, two journalistic giants, invited me to play for their famous Fleet Street Strollers in a friendly in Frank's home county of Derbyshire. I was torn between choosing football or cricket when I was leaving school, and fancied myself as the new Godfrey Evans of wicket keepers. I hadn't played for several years, but answered the call with some enthusiasm – particularly as Frank Nicklin had given me a nice little earner as a columnist with the *Sun*, for which he was a legendary sports editor.

It meant a round trip of three hundred miles from my home in Essex. I was on the road for eight hours and in between managed to get myself bowled first ball. What made it so amusing was that the following week the local Derbyshire newspaper was sent to me. It was one of those old-fashioned broadsheet papers, and they had got out their largest type and ran their headline across seven columns – as big as anything I had received as a footballer. It screamed, 'GREAVES FLOPS WITH A DUCK'. The price of fame!

 I went off playing the game after I had come face to face with former England left-arm fast bowler Fred Rumsey. He sent the ball whizzing so close to my nose that I could smell the leather, and from then on I decided to stick to spectating.

 Like I said, I wanted to be Godfrey Evans when I was a kid. That was in the days when you could play cricket and football, and there were great all-rounders like Denis Compton, Willie Watson and Arthur Milton.

When I got to Chelsea as a fifteen-year-old apprentice, Essex were showing interest in me. But Chelsea manager Ted Drake made it clear that the days of the football/cricket all-rounders were numbered, which was a bit selfish of him as he had played football for Arsenal and cricket for Hampshire.

It was Ted who told me the story of the all-rounder who always got a 100 against his name while playing cricket and was responsible for loads of goals as a footballer. Unfortunately for him, he was a bowler and a goalkeeper.

Trevor Bailey was another who was equally good at football, and squeezed in a distinguished amateur career between playing cricket for Essex and England.

I met Trevor many times at dinners and award ceremonies, and he told me of the day he bowled the great Australian Keith Miller for a first ball duck against Don Bradman's all-conquering 1948 tourists at Southchurch Park, Southend. That's the good news. The bad news is that the Aussies amassed an all-time record 712 runs in one day. They were all out before the close of play, the only time on that tour that every Australian batsman was dismissed.

Keith Miller, one of the game's great characters, later confessed that he had deliberately surrendered his wicket because he did not like the slaughter that was going on in the name of sport. He received an unusual honour for his non-scoring performance.

He was invited to join the Pygmalion Duck Club, formed by commentator John Arlott for batsmen considered to have collected 'a distinguished duck'.

 It was John Arlott who came up with one of the great commentating lines when England captain George Mann hit South African spinner Tufty Mann for six while Arlott was at the microphone. 'That,' said the master, 'is a true case of Mann's inhumanity to Mann.'

 And it was Keith Miller who – when captaining a team in Australia – led the players out for the start of play. One of the team ran up alongside him and said, 'Hey, skip, we've got twelve players.'

Without breaking step, Miller shouted over his shoulder: 'One of you f*** off!'

 Colin Ingleby-Mackenzie was surely the most laid-back captain of them all in the days when he skippered Hampshire. Asked on television what time he expected his players to be in bed, he said: 'I'm happy provided they are tucked up before ten o'clock . . . after all, the game starts at ten-thirty!' He made his comments on a kids' programme, which greatly upset the Establishment.

Known from then on as the 'breakfast-before-bed skipper', he was involved in another of those bizarre Dickie Bird incidents. This was in the days when Dickie was an opening bat for Leicestershire. As he prepared to face the first ball of the innings, Dickie thought he was hearing things. He felt sure he could hear a horse-racing commentary.

When he glanced to slip he saw Ingleby-Mackenzie with a transistor radio to his ear.

'Sorry about this, Dickie,' the Old Etonian said. 'Got a wad riding on the favourite.'

 Brian Close was the complete opposite to Ingers as a captain. He wanted blood, sweat and tears and would come down heavily on anybody not giving total concentration and effort. He led from the front, as anybody who saw him batting against the West Indies in the 1960s will remember. He stood up to those twin tornadoes Wes Hall and Charlie Griffith, letting the ball hit him on the body and carrying on as if he had been bitten by a gnat. His body was covered in bruises afterwards.

Ray Illingworth told this story about his fellow Yorkshireman: 'I was bowling for Yorkshire against Gloucestershire skipper Martin Young in a County match. Martin went down on one knee to play a sweep shot. He really middled the ball and it went like a bullet and hit Closie on the forehead straight between the eyes.

'Brian was fielding at short leg in the days before helmets. The ball bounced from his head back over the top of Martin Young, over the head of our wicket keeper Jimmy Binks and into the safe hands of Phil Sharpe at first slip.

'As Brian was being taken to the dressing room he was arguing that he should be credited with the catch!

Two famed and fearless Yorkshiremen, Ray Illingworth and Brian Close
(Neal Simpson/PA Photos).

'Martin Young went into the dressing room later, where Close was being stitched. The doctor said to Martin: "He'll be all right, and he should count himself lucky. I dread to think what would have happened if it had landed behind his ear."

'Close looked up from the treatment table nursing an egg-sized bump on his forehead and said to Young: "You would have been caught at cover instead of slip."'

They bred them tough in those days!

 Speaking as a proud Scot, I loved the greeting Bob Willis got when leading the England tour team to Australia in 1982. He had practised his opening words for the press, but was not quite prepared for the first question put to him by a hardnosed Aussie reporter: 'Welcome to Oz, Bob. What's it like to be leading the worst England team ever to visit these shores?'

Arthur Jepson, former professional footballer and cricketer, became an umpire who could match Dickie Bird as a character. While standing in a County match featuring Yorkshire, he had been irritated by the constant chatter of Geoff Boycott. A ball rapped Boycs on the pad, and he was convinced it was missing leg stump. Jepson begged to differ, and gave him out leg before.

Boycs glared at the umpire on his way to the pavilion. Jepson stared back and said, 'Now we'll get a bit of peace. I got rid of my dog for yapping. Now I've got rid of you.'

There is an even better comment from Jepson. This was during the 1971 Gillette Cup semi-final between Lancashire and Gloucestershire at Old Trafford. The game finished at 8.50 p.m. after Lancashire skipper Jack Bond politely asked Jepson about bad light. 'What's that up there?' asked Jepson, looking skywards. 'The moon,' replied Bond. 'Well, how far d'you want to see?' was Arthur's final word on the subject.

Australian Cec Pepper was credited with bringing sledging into English cricket when he played in the Lancashire League in the immediate post-war years. When he became an umpire, it was a classic case of poacher turned gamekeeper. He was a loud and aggressive appealer when bowling, badgering the umpire into raising a finger.

In one match, having had several appeals rejected by umpire George Long, Cec questioned his eyesight and parentage. At the end of the over, realising he had gone too far, Cec apologised profusely to the umpire.

Long said: 'Don't worry, Cec. Up here in Lancashire we like a man that speaks his mind.'

Feeling good and sensing he'd established a rapport

with the umpire, Cec resumed bowling and first ball in his next over hit the batsman on the pad. 'How's that?' he yelled at his new-found friend.

'Not out, you fat Australian bastard,' replied the umpire.

Years later, when umpiring, Cec was notorious for his sometimes outrageous behaviour. Brian 'Tonker' Taylor, then the Essex captain, once put in an official complaint to Lord's because Cec had farted continually throughout the day's play. The complaint read that 'the umpire obviously enjoyed it despite the protests of the players'.

 David Gower never gave the impression of thinking that cricket was a game of life or death. In one match batting for Leicestershire against Cambridge University, he decided to take runs only when he played the ball on the 'on' side. He kept the plan to himself, and his startled partner could not understand why he was continually sent back when the ball went from Gower's bat to the off side.

Gower later explained: 'To be honest, I found myself getting very bored out there so I devised this little private game to keep myself alert. The few times I miscued to the off side I just had to surrender the runs. My partner thought I had gone quite potty.'

England officials were convinced Gower had gone off his head when he and John Morris buzzed the pitch in a Tiger Moth during the England innings against Queensland at Carrara during the 1990–91 tour. Gower's only regret is that he did not put the finishing touch to the operation.

'I had wanted to bombard the pitch with water bombs,' he said, 'but it didn't work out.'

As the biplane flew low over the pitch, England batsmen Allan Lamb and Robin Smith looked up in amazement. Smith reacted by putting his bat to his shoulder and mimed taking rifle shots at the invader, not knowing it was his team-mates at the controls.

'Biggles' Gower and Morris were each fined £1000 by the MCC chiefs. In my opinion, Greavsie, they should have given them medals for bringing a smile to the face of sport.

 David has, of course, become an outstanding cricket commentator. He has yet to match the Brian Johnston classic when England were playing the West Indies at the Oval in 1976. He came out with this unforgettable line: 'The bowler's Holding the batsman's Willey.'

 Funniest cricketing commentary ever, Greavsie, also involved Brian Johnston. That was the day Ian Botham was out when Jonners and Jonathan Agnew were together at the *Test Match Special* microphone.

England were playing the West Indies at the Oval when Botham tried to play a hook shot off a Curtly Ambrose delivery, lost balance, and stepped over the stumps. His inner thigh brushed a bail and he had to walk.

Brian Johnston was reading out the scorecard summary when – at the mention of Botham's dismissal – Jonathan Agnew said as a throw-away, 'He just couldn't get his leg over.'

With Aggers giggling away in the background, Brian completely lost it and there was a full minute of barely suppressed laughter.

Ronnie Corbett summed up the reaction of listeners when he telephoned the BBC to say that he was driving along the motorway and laughed so much he had to pull over to the hard shoulder. It was an all-time classic.

 I love cool characters in sport, Saint, and there was nobody cooler in a crisis than Colin Cowdrey. He was one of the great gentlemen of sport, who would have been perfectly suited to the Edwardian days when sportsmanship was revered above uncouth thoughts of winning. Colin was given a violent introduction to cricket's ruthless modern era when he was called up as an emergency reinforcement at the age of forty-two on England's torrid tour of Australia in 1974–75.

Just four days after his arrival Down Under, Cowdrey was picked to play in the second Test on a lightning fast Perth pitch against the lethal Aussie fast bowling team of Dennis Lillee and Jeff Thomson. At the fall of the first England wicket, Cowdrey entered the cauldron to join Lancastrian David Lloyd in the middle.

He was greeted with a barrage of hostile bouncers, which whooshed past his ears, followed by a tirade of colourful language from Thomson.

At the end of the over, Lloyd strolled down the wicket to give some encouragement to his pilloried partner, only to be greeted by a grinning Cowdrey, who said as if stepping out of a P. G. Wodehouse page: 'I say, old chap, this is awfully good fun, don't you think!'

 I was at a sportsmen's dinner once where Jim Laker was guest speaker. He told the story of how – after he had taken the world record nineteen wickets against Australia in the 1956 Old Trafford Test – he was invited by a school sports master to present the end-of-term prizes. Laker said the headmaster, who knew nothing about cricket, introduced him like this: 'We are delighted to have with us Mr Baker, who has got nineteen tickets for the Old Trafford Test.'

 Few could match Freddie Trueman as an after-dinner speaker. I got to know him well over the years and used to love his stories, most of them true. He, for example, used to go into the dressing room of the opposition on the first morning of a match, look slowly around as if counting and say: 'Well, I can see at least five certain wickets for me today. I'll see thee out in t'middle.'

 I remember when the Leeds Test was abandoned because a 'Free George Davis' protestor had dug up the pitch, somebody asked Freddie what he would do to the culprits. 'I'd take them up to top of main stand and drop them one by one to the ground below,' he said in his thick Yorkshire accent. 'But I'd be fair with them. I'd have Keith Fletcher below trying to catch them.'

That was a cruel dig at Fletch, because he was always being barracked by the Headingley crowd for dropping catches.

 A Cambridge University batsman, having just been dismissed by a snorter from Freddie, acknowledged him with the compliment: 'That was a very good ball, Mr Trueman.' Freddie replied: 'Aye, and it were wasted on thee.'

 On the tour of Australia in 1962–63, the Reverend David Sheppard – I often met him later when he became Bishop of Liverpool – dropped several catches. 'Tell ye'sel it's Sunday, Rev,' Trueman shouted to him at slip, 'and keep tha bloody hands together!'

 Another true Freddie story was when an Aussie batsman edged him to first slip, and the ball shot right between Raman Subba Row's legs. At the end of the over, Subba ambled past Trueman and apologised sheepishly.

'I should've kept my legs together, Fred,' he said.

'Not thee, lad,' Freddie replied. 'Tha mother should've!'

Here's one I heard on a trip to Somerset, where Viv Richards is, of course, part of cricketing legend. A cocky young bowler made Richards play and miss with a superb outswinger in a County game. He then made the silly mistake of saying to Viv: 'It's red, round and weighs about five ounces.'

Next ball, Viv hits the ball out of the ground and replies, 'You know what it looks like, man. Go ahead and find it!'

The two South African-born Allans – Lamb and Donald – each had plenty to say for themselves during games. They came face to face when Donald was bowling for Warwickshire against Northants.

Lambie kept coming forward on his front foot, trying to hit Donald to the boundary. Donald dropped a couple short, and shouted down the wicket: 'Lambie, if you're so keen to drive hire yourself a car.'

The next ball was pitched right up, but Lambie was ready for it and hit a perfect cover drive to the ropes.

'Go and park that f****r!' he called back to Donald.

That great Australian wicket keeper Rodney Marsh used to try to upset the concentration of batsmen by saying to them as he crouched behind the stumps: 'How's your wife and my kids?'

Ian Botham was ready for him during a Test match, and replied: 'The wife's gorgeous, but the kids are retarded!'

Merv Hughes was king of the sledgers. He always found it easy to wind up Graeme Hick, the batsman he referred to as his bunny. He once made him play

Merv Hughes, always a dogged competitor (PA Photos).

and miss three times in succession, and shouted: 'Turn the bat over, mate, you'll find the instructions how to use it.'

In another match he said to Hick: 'In which part of the ground is your husband sitting? Does he play cricket as well?' Next ball, Merv clean bowled him.

 Mike Atherton was asked what Merv Hughes had been shouting at him when he was batting during a Test. The England skipper replied: 'The noise of the crowd was too great so I couldn't pick up every word. All I know is that every sentence finished with "arsewipe"!'

 I did some research to see where and when sledging started, Saint. One of your Scottish brethren was involved. It seems during the infamous Bodyline tour Down Under in 1932–33 England captain Douglas Jardine – at the crease, batting – complained to Aussie skipper Bill Woodfull that a slip fielder had sworn at him. Woodfull turned to his fielders and said: 'All right, which one of you bastards called this bastard a bastard?'

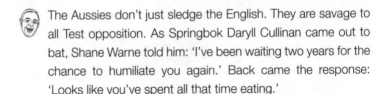

The Aussies don't just sledge the English. They are savage to all Test opposition. As Springbok Daryll Cullinan came out to bat, Shane Warne told him: 'I've been waiting two years for the chance to humiliate you again.' Back came the response: 'Looks like you've spent all that time eating.'

During the 1991 Test between Australia and Pakistan in Adelaide, Javed Miandad called Merv Hughes 'a fat bus conductor'. Merv dismissed him a couple of balls later, and as Javed walked past him on the way to the pavilion Merv shouted: 'Tickets please!'

Merv had a famous encounter with Vic Richards in Antigua, the home of the great man where he is the undisputed King. After each delivery Merv stood staring menacingly at the Master Blaster, trying to unsettle him. Eventually, Viv said: 'This is my island, man, my culture. Don't you be staring at me. In my culture we just bowl.' Merv had him caught in the next over, and said for Viv's hearing: 'In my culture, we just say f*** off!'

Aussie wicket keeper Ian Healy made it on to the front pages when a comment he made against Sri Lanka in a Sydney Test was clearly picked up and heard on television. The rather rotund Arjuna Ranatunga called for a runner, and Healey's comment was picked up by the stump mic: 'You don't get a runner for being an overweight, unfit, fat c**t.'

Aussie fast bowler Craig McDermott was bowled by Phil Tufnell on a dodgy wicket, and as he went past Tuffers he said: 'Your lot will be batting on this in a minute. They should book their hospital food now!'

 When Geoff Boycott made his entry into Test cricket in 1964 he wore glasses. As he took his guard ready to face the fearsome Garth McKenzie at Trent Bridge, Aussie skipper Bobby Simpson shouted from slip: 'Hey Garth, see if you can knock this four-eyed f*****'s glasses off.'

 Cleverest response I heard to sledging was when Steve Waugh's brother Mark said to England debutant Jimmy Ormond: 'What are you doing out here? There's no way you're good enough to play for England.' Ormond shut him up by replying: 'Well, at least I'm the best player in my own family!'

 Mike 'Gatt the Gut' Gatting was famous for his growing girth. Dennis Lillee said after a couple of his balls had been blocked, 'Hell, give us a chance, Gatt. Get out of the way so I can at least see the stumps.'

Then there was the frightening time when Dennis hit Derek Randall on the head with a bouncer. Mad-as-a-hatter Randall said, 'No good hitting me there, mate – nothing to damage.'

 When Mike Gatting was famously bowled by Shane Warne's first ball in a Test match in England, it's a little known fact that he should not even have been at the wicket. He had padded up quickly and gone in at number three because Robin Smith, due to go in first wicket down, had 'gone missing'. Smith,

Mike Gatting, Darren Gough and the umpire have a threesome encounter during a Test match (Chris Turvey/PA Photos).

nicknamed 'The Judge' by his England team-mates, was in fact detained in the toilet. The delay did not help Smith. He was soon back in the pavilion after also being bemused by Warne's prodigious spin.

Gatt, of course, was famed among his team-mates for his enormous appetite and his spreading waistline. Asked during a 1984 Test in India if he wanted Gatting wider at slip, bowler Chris Cowdrey said to skipper David Gower: 'Any wider and he'll burst!'

 I once took part in a sports forum at an American Air Force base and we were asked to give a summary of the rules of cricket. This is what the panel came up with:

- You have two sides, one out in the field and one in.

- Each man that's in the side that's in goes out, and when he's out he comes in and the next man goes in until he's out.

- When they are all out, the side that's out comes in and the side that's been in goes out and tries to get those coming in, out.

- Sometimes you get men still in and not out.

- When a man goes out to go in, the men who are out try to get him out, and when he is out he goes in and the next man in goes out and goes in.

- There are two men called umpires who stay out all the time and they decide when the men who are in are out.

- When both sides have been in and all the men have been out, and both sides have been out twice after all the men have been in, including those who are not out, that is the end of the game.

For some reason, Saint, the Americans said they were still baffled by the game!

 And to wind up this cricketing chapter here is a collection that we've gathered of novel ways that batsmen have found to get themselves out . . .

- Leicestershire wicketkeeper Thomas Sidwell was one not out overnight against Surrey at the Oval in 1921. Making his way to the ground the next morning he managed to get himself lost on the London Underground. He arrived too late to bat, and it went down in the scorebook as 'T. Sidwell, absent, lost on tube.'

- Alf Gover had just finished a spell of bowling for Surrey and went to short leg, holding his sweater. He was just pulling it over his head as Jim Laker bowled to Rodney Exton. Gover was unsighted as Exton hit a shot in his direction. The ball hit his legs and he instinctively caught it between his thighs, his sweater still over his head!

- New Zealander Martin Donnelly, playing for Warwickshire, was hit on a foot by a ball from Middlesex spinner Jack Young in 1948. The ball looped into the air over Donnelly's head, landed two feet behind the stumps and then spun back and hit his wicket.

- Keith Miller had made up his mind to try to hit Norman Yardley for six at Headingley during the 1948 England–Australia Test. Yardley anticipated his intentions and bowled the ball wide outside leg stump. Miller took a huge swing, overbalanced and the ball hit the bottom edge of his bat. The ball spun back behind him, whacked wicket-keeper Godfrey Evans on the head and was then spectacularly caught by Bill Edrich, who threw himself full length at first slip to hold the ball. Miller laughed all the way back to the pavilion.

- A ball from Athol Rowan ballooned up off the glove of Len Hutton during the Fifth Test between England and South Africa at the Oval in 1951. As wicketkeeper Russell Endean reached for the ball, Hutton fended it away from the stumps with his bat and was given out for obstructing the field.

- Surrey's Alec Bedser bowled Derbyshire batsman Alan Revill a sharp lifter at the Oval in 1953. Revill was struck sharply on the hand. As he instinctively shook his right hand in pain, his glove flew off and dislodged a bail. Judged still to be in the process of 'playing at the ball', he was given out 'hit wicket'.

- Peter May was run out in peculiar circumstances while batting for Surrey against Glamorgan at the Oval in 1957. He played uppishly towards wide mid-on, set off on a run and then saw Glamorgan fielder Bernard Hedges running in to take the catch. May took it that the ball had been caught and started off on the slow walk back to the pavilion. Behind his back, Hedges had dropped the catch. He then picked the ball up and lobbed it to Glamorgan skipper Wilfred Wooller, who broke the wicket. May didn't see any of this and thought he had been caught out.

- In a Sheffield Shield match at Adelaide in 1969 a Greg Chappell delivery to John Inverarity dramatically changed direction in mid-air, suddenly nose-diving to flatten the stumps. Completely bewildered, Inverarity started to walk to the pavilion but was then recalled. Umpire Colin Egar had signalled a dead ball. A swallow, now also dead and lying some yards behind the wicket, was revealed as the cause for the freak dismissal.

- Non-striker Andrew Hilditch retrieved a wayward return and handed the ball to Sarfraz Nawaz during an Australia–Pakistan Test in 1979. Sarfraz appealed and Hilditch was given out 'handled ball'.

- Former Warwickshire and England batsman Mike Smith was facing a ball in a County match against Hampshire at Edgbaston in 1962 when a sudden gust of wind whipped his cap off his head. It fell on to the stumps, and he was given out 'hit wicket'.

- Close fielder Allan Lamb jumped to avoid a crashing shot from Wayne Phillips off the bowling of Phil Edmonds in the England–Australia Test at Edgbaston in 1985. The ball rebounded off Lamb's boot to be caught by David Gower.

- Graham Gooch jabbed down late on an express delivery from Merv Hughes during the England–Australia Test at Old Trafford in 1993. As the ball ricocheted off the pitch and lobbed menacingly towards the stumps, Gooch used his hand to push it away. The Aussie fielders appealed and Dickie Bird gave him out. The scorer, for the first time in a Test, wrote of an Englishman: 'G. Gooch, out, handled ball.'

- Michael Vaughan, playing for England against India in Bangalore in 2001, missed a sweep shot off Sarandeep Singh and the ball got trapped beneath him. Even though the ball wasn't heading towards his stumps, he instinctively brushed it away. The Indians appealed, as was their right, and Vaughan was sent packing, much to the disgust of his captain, Nasser Hussain, who claimed it was 'against the spirit of the game'.

- Andrew Symonds, batting for Australia against Sri Lanka in Melbourne in 2006, hammered a shot down the wicket that looked a certain four. The ball hit his partner Michael Clarke low on his pad and the ball flew to Dilshan at wide mid-on. He held on for a most improbable catch. As Symonds departed for the pavilion he mimed as if he was sinking a pint to Clarke, meaning that he owed him an after-match drink.

Saint's Cricket Jokes

An expectant father rang the maternity hospital to see how his wife was getting on. By mistake he dialled the number for Lord's. 'What's the latest?' he asked. 'It's looking good,' came the reply. 'We've got two out already and hope to have the rest out before lunch. The last one was a duck.'

* * *

A renowned England slip specialist, famous for his safe hands, was walking down the high street when he approached a building that was on fire. He was just in time to see a young child jump from a second-storey window.

Racing forward, he caught the child and then, from habit, tossed it in the air.

Greavsie's Cricket Jokes

This story has been put around as involving a notoriously hot-tempered Australian fast bowler, but I am assured it's a joke. The opening bowler was hurling the ball down but getting nowhere against a batsman who was as wide as he was tall. The bowler, frustrated, decides to try to niggle him with a verbal insult. 'How did you get as fat as that?' he asks the batsman.

'It's your wife's fault,' replied the batsman. 'Everytime I screw her she gives me a biscuit.'

* * *

The young England debutant batsman was shaking with nerves as he faced the Australian pace attack of Lillee and Thomson, and could hardly lay bat to ball. During a break in the blitz, he mumbled nervously to wicket-keeper Rodney Marsh, 'Well, I expect you've seen worse players.'

Marsh did not respond, and skipper Greg Chappell at first slip shouted: 'He said I expect you've seen worse players.'

'I heard him the first time,' said Marsh. 'I'm still trying to think of one.'

The Talk of Cricket

Ian Chappell

A main advantage England have is that when Phil Tufnell is bowling he isn't fielding.

Mike Brearley

Playing against a team captained by Ian Chappell turns a cricket match into gang warfare.

John Warr

Denis Compton was the only batsman who would call his partner for a run and wish him luck at the same time.

Dennis Lillee

When I was bowling purposeful bouncers my aim was to hit the batsman in the ribcage, and I wanted it to hurt him so much that he did not want to face me any more.

Dickie Bird

I am only happy when I am standing in the middle of a cricket ground.

Richie Benaud

Batting is a trial before an eleven-man jury.

BBC Radio announcer

Yorkshire 232 all out, Hutton ill . . . I'm sorry, Hutton 111.

Australian radio announcer

Glenn McGrath joins Craig McDermott and Paul Reiffel in a three-ponged prace attack.

Tony Greig, in a live Test broadcast:

In the back of Hughes's mind must be the thought that he will dance down the piss and mitch one.

Rodney Hogg, remembering the majesty of Viv Richards:

I bounced a cricket ball off his cheek and waited for him to fall down. He just stared at me, carried on chewing gum and hit my next ball for six, twenty-four rows back.

Denis Norden, king of the comedy scriptwriters:

October is a funny kind of month. For the cricket fanatic, it's when you realise that your wife left you in May.

5) JOLLY GREEN GIANTS

 We are so lucky, Greavsie, to still be active sportsmen long after we hung up our shooting boots. I'm referring, of course, to our joint love of golf. My wife, Betsy, is a single handicap player, and the two of us have travelled the world playing the finest courses and enjoying the greatest views on earth.

 My wife, Irene, doesn't play, but likes golf because it gets me out from under her feet after our fifty years together. We can both do quite a bit of name-dropping. I'll let you go first.

 Well, there was the time, for instance, when I made an eagle to Nick Faldo's birdie on the eighteenth at Gleneagles.

It happened in a pro-am the week before the Scottish Open. Faldo played with the blinkers on, hardly acknowledging the existence of any of the other three players in the group. That was his right, but his arrogant attitude generated a lot of unnecessary tension, made worse by one of our partners spraying the ball everywhere bar the fairway.

When I stood on the eighteenth tee I was determined to try to finish with a flourish. I put a decent drive down the middle of the fairway, but my second shot drifted into some short rough about ninety yards from the green. As I addressed the ball I felt confident I could make the green and be in with a chance of putting for a birdie four.

There was a big stand overlooking the green, with quite a lot of spectators watching out for celebrities. It was wonderful for me to hear a smattering of applause as my ball rolled on to the green towards the flag, and this became a roar as it disappeared down the hole.

Of all my times playing golf – and they would have been a lot more if Bill Shankly had not been so anti the game – this was my big Walter Mitty moment.

Naturally, I waved to the still applauding crowd when I fished my ball out of the hole. Faldo duly put his putt down for a birdie. He then allowed himself one of the few things he said all through the round: 'Lucky bastard.'

 Faldo was notorious for his sharp tongue and insular attitude when he was competing at the highest level, but he seems to have loosened up a bit since following a career as a golf commentator in the United States.

You surprise me, Saint, when you say that Shanks was anti-golf.

 He hated the game, and would get hopping mad if he found out that any of his players had been near a course in the week of a game. Shanks reckoned that walking the course stiffened the calves and made the legs heavy and tired. He was not a very good advert for the home of golf!

I had another uncomfortable round with Faldo in a BBC celebrity event at Turnberry. I was grouped with my old chum

Jimmy Tarbuck in a foursome featuring Faldo and the great American Johnny Miller.

You'd think this would be golf heaven. Tarby and I were looking forward to it like kids anticipating Christmas, and as we walked on to the first tee we were laughing happily and full of the joys of spring.

We were greeted by Johnny Miller scowling in our direction. 'Too much laughing on the tee,' he snapped, as he reached for his driver.

Tarby being Tarby, he could not resist a response. 'It's what is known as having a sense of humour,' he said. Suddenly the temperature dropped to freezing point.

Faldo was again as miserable as sin, and what should have been an enjoyable occasion was weighed down with tension that even one of Britain's funniest men could not lighten.

Another time I partnered none other than Sir Sean Connery in a pro-celebrity tournament at Turnberry, and together we beat the pairing of Lee Trevino and Sandy Lyle. Sandy Lyle was everything that Faldo wasn't. He was open, friendly, helpful and encouraging. Trevino was all I imagined, talking non-stop, joking with the crowd and making it an amusing as well as rewarding experience

Sir Sean was deadly serious about his golf, but had to laugh at this joke from Trevino: James Bond walks into a bar and takes a seat next to a very attractive woman. He gives her a quick glance, and then casually looks at his watch for a moment. The woman notices the unusual watch and says: 'I don't think I've ever seen a wristwatch quite like that.' Bond replies: 'My gadget-maker Q has just given it to me and I am testing it.' Intrigued, the woman says, 'What's so special about it?' Bond explains: 'It uses ultra-magnetic waves to talk to me telepathically.' The lady asks, 'What's it telling you now?' 'Well,' says James, 'it has revealed that you're not wearing any panties.' The woman giggles and replies, 'Well, it must be broken because I AM wearing panties!' Bond frowns, taps his watch and says, 'Bloody thing's an hour fast.'

One of my most memorable golfing moments was when I played a round with Seve Ballesteros in Spain. The great Spaniard was somewhere near his peak, and agreed to a TV interview while we went round the course.

I sliced my drive off the first tee, and Seve bent over laughing. 'Yimmy,' he said, 'I theenk you better stick to football.'

He then knelt down, took his driver and smashed the ball 270 yards straight down the middle of the fairway.

To make me feel better about my wayward drive, he told me a story while walking down the fairway about the worst hole of his life.

'Early in my career,' he said, 'I was very cocky and boasted that I would never ever take double figures on a hole. The very next day in the Spanish Open I hooked my drive out of bounds at the par five ninth hole. I then did the same thing with my next drive, and by the time I found the fairway I had five shots to my name.

'My sixth shot went into a water hazard, and I put the replacement ball into the bunker. I was finally on the green in nine, and two putted for an eleven. It taught me that in future I should be careful about what I said!'

Between us, Greavsie, we know enough golf stories to fill this book. I loved the one about the Hungarian immigrant Julius Boros, who won the US Open. When he reached fifty, keen angler Boros was asked if he was contemplating retirement. 'What would I do with myself if I retired?' he asked. 'All I'm interested in is fishing and golfing.'

I laughed when Maurice Flitcroft, a forty-six-year-old crane driver from Barrow-in-Furness, carded a record 121 strokes in the first qualifying round for the British Open at Formby in Lancashire, and the Open championship committee immediately tightened their entry rules. Maurice, who had given hope to all rabbits, told the press: 'I could have done with a bit more practice.'

I was once a World Cup winner, but it was on the golf course rather than the football pitch. It was in a tournament staged in Mendoza during the 1978 World Cup finals, and the European media were invited to take part. I was loaned a set of clubs, and went round the fine course with a young Argentinian player. Afterwards at the awards dinner, the MC announced the prizes. 'And the winner of the media section,' he said, 'is Ian St John of ITV, London. Well, as you can imagine, I was chuffed. I went up to receive the trophy and made a gracious victory speech. At the bar later, I asked one of the tournament organisers how many of my peers I had beaten to the prize. He seemed reluctant to answer, but I pressed him. 'Well,' he said, 'in truth you were the only entrant . . .' I wish I'd never asked.

It could have been worse, Saint. You could have come second.

Two unbelievable cow stories – the first years ago when Kent club professional Bill Robinson sliced a drive off the eighteenth tee. The ball smacked a cow in the head, killing it stone dead.

There was a happier ending to a cow story in Texas. A ball slashed off the first was assumed lost, until it was found – wait for it – stuck in the arse of a grazing cow. If that had been me, I'd have claimed a hole in one.

The legendary Silver Scot Tommy Armour holds the record for most shots on a single hole on the US PGA tour. He took twenty-three during the Shawnee Open in 1927. Just a week earlier he had won the US Open. It is claimed Tommy was trying to see if he could get the ball to skim across a lake. He might have been able to walk on water, but his balls kept sinking!

Armour was an astonishing character – one of the finest bridge players in the world, a classical violinist and a war hero. He served as a machine gunner with the Black Watch in the Great War, and he once single-handedly captured an enemy tank, an act of heroics that included having to strangle a German officer. He was presented with a special bravery medal by King George V.

After the war he won more than forty tournaments including the US Open, the PGA in 1930 and the Open at Carnoustie in 1931 – all this despite having lost an eye in battle and having metal plates in his head and in his left arm. He was a true miracle man of golf.

On top of everything else, Tommy was a notorious womaniser, could drink most people under the table, was a born raconteur and a dedicated gambler. He also had one hell of a temper. Once, after poor putting had cost him a tournament he had backed himself to win, he threw his putter out of the window of a train as it crossed the Forth Bridge.

 Here's something you'll never read about tortoise-pace Bernhard Langer. Mark Calcavecchia and John Daly were both fined by the US Tour for playing too quickly. They completed the final round in the Tournament Players' Championship in two hours and three minutes. Daly fired an eighty and Calcavecchia an eighty-one. The suggestion was they were not showing the event the respect it deserved.

Even in Majors, Daly takes an average twenty seconds per putt. Langer's average when he was a regular on the Tour was ninety seconds. Lanny Wadkins said that he could grow a moustache in the time it took Bernhard to line up a putt.

This is a true story about a member of a golf club in the North-West who sadly passed on to the great golf course in the sky. He was renowned as a wonderful straight hitter who always played it straight down the middle, and won many tournaments with his uncanny accuracy. In his will he asked for his ashes to be scattered on his beloved first fairway. The club staged a special ceremony, and the current captain took on the job of scattering the ashes. As he opened the urn a sudden gust of wind took hold of the ashes and blew them off the fairway, where they came to rest in a huge bush. It was the only time he had ever been out of bounds.

It's impossible to know all the rules in golf. Craig Stadler thought he knew them all, but discovered a new one in the 1987 San Diego Open at Torrey Pines. His ball had landed under a bush in a mud patch. Rather than pick and drop, Craig decided to go on his knees to play the ball out. To save getting mud on his trousers, he put down a towel and knelt on it and proceeded to play his shot. A sharp-eyed 'know-all' viewer – watching on television – telephoned the tournament organisers and reported Stadler for breaking the rules. Putting the towel down constituted 'building a stance', and Stadler was disqualified.

Stadler, the Walrus Man, was once asked why he was

using a new putter. 'Because the old one', he said, 'didn't float very well.'

 Jack Nicklaus, the Golden Bear, was being showered with praise by a fawning television interviewer, who gushed: 'You are such a spectacular player, Jack. Your name is synonymous with the game of golf, and there is nobody who can match your fantastic Majors record. How do you know your way around a golf course so well?'

'The holes', Jack replied, 'are numbered.'

 Yes, Jack could sometimes be a rascal with his replies when he was asked daft questions. I heard him being interviewed during one of the Majors back in the early 90s and he was asked: 'Tell me, Jack, why do you tee up your balls so high?'

'After many years of experience,' Jack replied, 'I find that air offers less resistance than dirt.'

 Colin Montgomerie is one of the greatest golfers we have ever produced, but is never given the credit he deserves on the other side of the pond. He gets unmerciful stick from the galleries in the States. I just wish he could win a Major to stuff all their criticism down their throats. He had to go through all that nonsense of being dubbed Mrs Doubtfire. This was after the following exchange between Colin and a fan during one of the US Opens . . .

'Hey, Monty.'

Montgomerie kept his head down.

'Monty,' the fan yelled again. And again.

Montgomerie didn't look up until the fan adopted the polite approach.

'Excuse me, *Mister* Montgomerie.'

Colin Montgomerie has a great golf swing but also mood swings (PA Photos).

Finally, Colin made eye contact, at which the fan said to arguably the finest golfer Britain has produced in the last quarter of a century, 'That's a nice pair of tits you've got there.'

That's shameful behaviour. I know where I would have stuck my driver if I'd been in Colin's shoes.

 Monty has been his own worst enemy with his mood swings, and losing his temper when things are not going right. But I agree with you that he has been one of our great golf masters.

Perhaps he could take a tip from the old golf giant Sam Snead. He said that if he felt he was allowing tension into his game, he would hum 'The Blue Danube'. He said it helped him restore his swing and rhythm and stopped him thinking bad thoughts.

For Colin, how about 'The Flower of Scotland'?

David Feherty, who was a top-flight pro on the European circuit, is now a leading commentator in the USA where he is known as the leader of the Tiger Woods fan club. A great raconteur, David told this after-dinner story that captures the magic of Tiger: 'I'm walking down the eighteenth fairway at Firestone Country Club with Ernie Els and Tiger, who has popped up a three-wood about forty yards behind Ernie into some wet, nasty, horrible, six-inch rough.

'Tiger's cursing and taking clumps out of Ohio with his three-wood. And, of course, we're not showing this on TV because we want to be able to interview him later. Ernie and I walk past Tiger's ball, and it is truly buried.

'Ernie is tied with Tiger and he's in the middle of the fairway. I'm standing with Ernie and my microphone is open. Ken Venturi [in the CBS booth] sends it to me and I say, "Tiger's got 184 yards with two big red oaks overhanging the green. He's got absolutely nothing. With a stick of dynamite and a sand wedge I might be able to move this ball fifty yards. Steve Williams [Woods' caddie] tells me [with a hand signal] that he's using a pitching wedge."

'Tiger takes his swing. Every muscle in his body is flung at the ball. It looks like he's torn his nutsack. The divot went as far as I could hit the ball. I've got my microphone at my mouth thinking, what the hell was that! The ball sails over the trees, lands behind the hole and backs up to about six feet from the flag. I open my microphone and Ernie turns and says, "F*** me!"

'My producer comes on in my earpiece and says, "Was that Ernie?" I say yes. He says, "Fair enough."

'I could have described that shot for fifteen minutes and not done as good a job as Ernie did with two words. This is one of the best players in the world talking, and you wanna know how good Tiger is? Ask Ernie Els.'

Great story. I've got another true story from American television. During a PGA golf tournament a commentator offered an exclusive insight into Arnold Palmer's game. 'One of the reasons Arnie is playing so well,' he told viewers, 'is that he has a superstition. Before each tee shot, his wife has to take out his balls and kiss them . . .' There was a slight pause followed by: 'Oh my God, what have I just said?'

It was Arnie Palmer who, when asked by a novice how he could get ten shots off his score, replied: 'Get yourself a good eraser.'

 I have to keep my temper in check on the course at times, but I am mild-mannered compared with former US Open champion Tommy Bolt. His violent temper earned him the nickname Thunderbolt. One of his most publicised outbursts came in the US Open at Denver when he mis-hit a shot into the pond at the twelfth.

He had a heated argument with a US PGA official as to where he should place the ball for his penalty shot, and this so upset his concentration that he three putted the next hole, bogeyed the following and hit two drives off the eighteenth tee into a lake.

By then, Bolt was in his most thunderous mood, and at the end of the round he swung his driver round his head and sent it spinning into the lake. A small boy came racing out of the crowd, dived into the lake and came out triumphantly holding the driver.

Bolt's caddie walked forward to receive it, but to the cheers of the gallery, the boy side-stepped him and raced off into the distance clutching his prize.

 Another famous anecdote about Tommy was when he once found himself playing with a caddie who used to irritate his golfers by constantly chattering. Before they teed off, Bolt ordered him not to say anything unless asked – and then to answer only 'yes' or 'no'.

On the fourth hole, Bolt found his ball lying next to a tree and was required to hit under a branch, over a lake and on to the green. He got down on his knees and looked through the trees, sizing up the shot.

'What do you think?' he asked the caddie. 'Five-iron?'

'No, Mr Bolt,' the caddie said.

'What do you mean, not a five-iron?' Bolt snorted. 'Well, I reckon it is. Watch this shot.'

The caddie rolled his eyes. 'No, Mr Bolt.'

Bolt ignored him and hit the ball well, placing it within a couple of feet of the flag. He then turned to his caddie and handed him the five-iron. 'Now what do you think about that?' he asked. 'I give you permission to talk now.'

'Mr Bolt,' the caddie replied, 'that wasn't your ball.'

 Bolt gave some advice that all hot-tempered golfers would do well to take on board. He said that if you are going to throw your club, make sure you throw it in a forward direction. 'There's nothing more humiliating,' said Tommy, 'than having to go back for your club.'

John Daly, the Wild Thing of golf, didn't take this advice when he threw his putter in temper in the Australian PGA tournament in Queensland. He threw it sideways into a lake, and was heavily fined.

But the fine was peanuts compared with the £32 million he admits having gambled away during his career.

 Jesper Parnevik was another with a short fuse. The Swede was so angry with himself over a round he played at Merion that he dived into the duck pond alongside the eighteenth green. But his temper was controlled compared with his countryman Anders Forsbrand. He has been seen attacking greens with his club after missed putts, and several clubs have been snapped over his knee.

Tony Johnstone, of Zimbabwe, can also let fly and once in a temper snapped a golf club, which was tossed into a bin in the locker room. Britain's Mark Roe, winner of the 1994 French Open, fished out the club and had it mounted on a board for a special presentation ceremony.

The best throwing story I heard concerned former England cricket captain Brian Close, who was a single handicap golfer whether playing right- or left-handed. He once in temper threw his entire golf bag into a lake and stomped off towards the clubhouse. Ten minutes later he came back in search of the bag. 'My car keys are in the pocket,' he was heard to mumble.

 Lee Trevino was full of stories when I played with him. He said he took part in a charity event in Las Vegas and quickly realised the organisers had given him a novice caddie. 'I drove off from the first tee,' said Lee, 'and asked how far I was from the green. "About three blocks," came the reply.'

 Prince Andrew has caught the golf bug, and I wonder whether he will become as fanatical a player as his great-uncle, the Duke of Windsor, who – when Prince of Wales – was coached by 'The Maestro' Henry Cotton. Henry was close friends with Chelsea manager Ted Drake and I often met him at Stamford Bridge. He once told me: 'The Prince of Wales could easily have been a scratch golfer. I recall an incident when an Irish caddie made him shake with laughter during a round that was played at Gleneagles. The Prince was crouching down trying to work out his line for a long putt, and he asked his caddie's advice. "If I were you, sir," he said in a thick Irish accent, "I would hit it slightly straight."'

Ian Woosnam was having one of his less illustrious rounds early in his professional career. He had spent more time in the woods than David Bellamy. He was struggling to break eighty and there was no chance of him making the cut. As he stood ankle-deep in the rough at the seventeeth, he asked his caddie: 'What should I take now?' Back came the reply: 'The next train home.'

Max Faulkner, the colourful 1951 Open champion, employed a regular caddie nicknamed 'Mad Mac', who was, to say the least, somewhat eccentric. He wore a raincoat but no shirt, and he always studied the greens through binoculars from which the lenses had been removed.

Faulkner was teeing off in a domestic tournament when he noticed his caddie was swaying as if in a strong wind. 'Are you all right, Mac?' asked Max.

'I'm as trim as a daisy,' the caddie replied in a slurred voice. 'I've just polished off a bottle of brandy, and I'll start on another one when you've won this tournament.'

Faulkner birdied the hole in three, and then looked around for the flag. His caddie was flat out on the side of the green, clasping the flag in his arms.

Max replaced the flag in the hole, and then half carried and half dragged the caddie behind a gorse bush where he left him sleeping like a baby.

Doug Sanders will always be remembered for missing a sitter of a putt that would have won him the British Open in 1970 – he

Sir Ian Botham joins golf
partner Ian Woosnam in this
Little and Large line-up
(Andrew Milligan/PA Photos).

went on to lose the play-off against Jack Nicklaus. He also had
putting problems in the 1968 Masters when he played magnificent golf everywhere but on the green. At the end of the round,
his caddie Walter 'Cricket' Pritchett said: 'Nice work, Mr Doug.
You've just managed to turn a perfect sixty-four into a seventy-
two!'

 US Tour professional Mark Brooks marked his ball on the
green during a Las Vegas tournament and then picked it up
and tossed it to his caddie for cleaning. The caddie missed
it and the ball splashed into the man-made lake alongside
the green. The rules are that you must finish the hole with
the ball you started. Brooks was in no mood to forfeit
penalty points, and so he took off his shoes, socks, shirt

and rolled up his trousers and waded into the lake looking for his ball. He fished out a dozen balls, but not one of them belonged to him. You could say he had thrown the game.

American professional Harry Gonder set out to prove a theory that a scratch golfer should be able to land a hole in one in a given number of shots. He filled a bucket with balls and, with two club officials in tow as witnesses, he went to the tee at the course's 160-yard third hole. He estimated that it would take no longer than half an hour for him to get an ace.

He bombarded the flag with balls, and came within fifteen inches of the hole with his eighty-sixth shot. Harry took a break for lunch after failing to get the elusive hole in one with 941 shots. His fifty-fifth shot on his restart came to rest just three inches from the flag, but still no ace.

He continued right on through the afternoon and long into the night, but finally had to concede defeat at three o'clock the next morning after playing for more than sixteen hours and in the glare of car headlights.

By the time he gave up, Harry had played a total of 1817 shots without getting a hole in one. Three months later, playing in competition, he holed out with a seven iron.

The wonderful thing about golf, Saint, is that novices can enjoy it as much as the scratch players. I was told this lovely story by a middle-aged lady who came to one of my road shows: 'My husband was trying to persuade me to take up golf, and one afternoon he talked me into walking around the course with him. As we arrived, four women were preparing to leave the first tee after driving off.

'They proceeded down the fairway chatting merrily and

after about sixty yards the first woman took her second shot. Within the next few yards, two more women took their second shots. The fourth member appeared to be searching for her ball, and then had a conversation with her friends.

'She then started to walk back towards the tee, hauling her trolley.

'"Oh no," she said with a giggle, while reaching down into her bag for a ball. "I've just realised that I was so busy talking that I forgot to drive off."

'Watching these women convinced me I could not possibly do worse, and they were enjoying themselves so much. I have since had years of playing the wonderful game.'

 An old friend passed on this true story: 'I arranged a game at our local club with my father, who was well into his eighties and becoming somewhat absent-minded. He had been a low handicap golfer years earlier, and had been the one who introduced me to the great game.

'We were off to a good start to the day when we went to the boot of the car to find that instead of packing his golf clubs he had put in a bag of gardening tools.

'We hired a set of clubs for him and then started our round. On the first tee Dad hooked his drive into the trees on the left. I went off to take my second shot, and then went back to help him look for his ball.

'When I reached the woods he was nowhere to be seen.

'I waved through the following four-ball and then hurried back to the clubhouse to see if Dad was there. There was no sign of him, and as I returned towards the first fairway I caught sight of him. He was preparing to putt on the eighteenth green!

'He had come out of the woods on the other side where the eighteenth fairway ran parallel with the first.

"What kept you?' he asked. 'Did you lose your ball?'

'I could not talk for laughing. He had completed the course in four shots!'

It is what is known as an under-Pa story, Greavsie!

Saint's Golf Joke

A golfer, playing a round by himself, is about to tee off, when the club's assistant professional comes up to him. He is desperate for money.

'Wait, before you tee off,' the assistant says, 'I have something really sensational to show you! It's a wonder ball that you can have for just a fiver.'

The golfer, annoyed to be interrupted, says: 'A fiver for a ball? You must be joking.'

'But there's no other ball like it,' says the assistant. 'You can never lose it!'

'What d'you mean,' the golfer says mockingly, 'you can never lose it? What if you hit it into the lake?'

'No problem,' says the assistant. 'It floats, and it detects where the shore is, and heads towards it.'

'Well, what if you hit it deep into the woods?'

'Easy,' says the assistant. 'It is programmed to let out a beeping sound, so you can find it even in the thickest rough or in heavy undergrowth.'

'Okay,' says the golfer, finally impressed. 'But what if you're playing a late round and it suddenly gets dark?'

'No problem, sir, it glows in the dark! I'm telling you, you can never lose this golf ball. And all I want for it is a fiver.'

The golfer takes a five pound note out of his wallet, and he is about to hand it over when he says: 'Just one question – where did you get it?'

'I found it.'

Greavsie's Golf Jokes

The police are called to a house where they find a man standing by the side of the lifeless body of a woman. He is holding a seven iron in his hand.

The police officer asks: 'Is this your wife, sir?'

'Yes, it is.'

'Did you hit her with that golf club?'

'Yes, yes, I did.' The man stifles a sob, drops the club, and puts his hands to his head.

'How many times did you hit her?'

The man looks off, mentally counting. 'I don't know . . . Five, six, seven . . . Put me down for a five.'

* * *

A golfer was having a nightmare round, spending more time in the bunker than Hitler and ploughing up the fairway.

Hacking his way down the eighteenth, he was 120 yards from the green and asked his cynical caddie: 'Do you think I can get there with a seven iron?'

The caddie replied, 'Eventually.'

The Talk of Golf

Walter Hagen

Never hurry, never worry and be sure to smell the flowers along the way.

Bobby Jones

Golf is a game played on a five-inch course – the distance between your ears.

Lee Trevino

Golf is the most fun I've had with my clothes on.

Sir Winston Churchill

Golf is an ineffectual attempt to direct an uncontrollable sphere into an inaccessible hole with instruments ill adapted for the purpose.

Mark Twain

Golf is a good walk spoiled.

Jackie Gleason

If I put the ball where I can see it, I can't reach it. If I put it where I can reach it, I can't see it.

Bob Charles

It's a big advantage to be left-handed. Nobody knows enough about your swing to be able to mess you up with advice.

Doug Sanders

I think those golfers who look as if they got dressed in the dark should be penalised two strokes for offending the public eye.

Tom Watson

Muirfield without a wind is like a lady undressed. There's no challenge.

Sam Snead

I once shot a wild, charging elephant in Africa that kept coming at me until it dropped dead at my feet. I wasn't a bit scared. It takes a four-foot putt to scare me to death.

A. A. Milne

Golf is so popular simply because it is the best game in the world at which to be bad.

Arnold Palmer

What other people may find in poetry or art museums, I find in the flight of a good drive.

6 YOU CAN'T BEAT A GOOD RUCK

So come on, Greavsie, time to come clean. You startled me in the opening chapter by saying rugby has taken over from football as your favourite sport. Why?

That would take another book to explain, Saint. But briefly, I think it's as much a case of attitudes as spectacle. Since football ceased to become a game of true physical contact, players have lost a lot of their bottle. There are many of them, particularly high-paid mercenaries in the Premier League, who cry to the referee at the hint of a tackle. Rugby remains a real man's game.

The game has become a much better spectacle since they changed a few of the rules. For instance, players used to be able to lie on the ball for as long as they liked and it became one long ruck, with few decent handling movements. Now they have to make instant release and teams are encouraged to run. The sight of a good three-quarter movement, with dummies, acceleration, side-stepping and slick passing, can be as exciting as anything you see in sport.

And I'll tell you this, Saint, I have not seen anything in any sport to match the drama and excitement of Jonny Wilkinson's last-minute drop goal that clinched the World Cup for England in 2003.

Yeah, I guessed you'd come up with that one. I'll tell you when I thought it was a great game to watch – the summer of 1995, the World Cup semi-final. Jonah Lomu was cutting through the England defence like a knife through butter. He ran in four tries, and crashed through the tackles of players like Tony Underwood and fullback Mike Catt.

When I was researching for our book, I discovered that Jonah had been wound up before the match when he read a quote allegedly coming from Underwood in which he said he would take Lomu out of the game by running around him.

Jonah said later: 'As I went in for one of my tries I took Underwood out to the sideline, shaking off his tackle. When he got up I said to him after touching down, "If you've got any more, man, you'd better bring it on."'

The tackle that everybody remembers was when Lomu appeared to walk over fullback Mike Catt on his way to scoring. It was something of a mismatch because Jonah the Whale had a five-stone weight advantage. Jonah admitted that if he hadn't been held up by Catt he wouldn't have been able to stay on his feet. By being brave – or foolish – enough to try to tackle him face on, Mike had turned himself into a doormat.

Anyway, going back to that Wilkinson kick . . . it was a replica of what Rob Andrew produced in the last seconds against Australia (again) in the quarter-finals of the 1995 World Cup. England manager Jack Rowell summed up the euphoria perfectly. 'People – including myself – jumped

Jonah Lomu making a meal of
the England defence during
the 1995 World Cup
(Tony Marshall/PA Photos).

ten feet in the air,' he said, 'and when they came down
they were crying.'

 Okay, you've made your point. England have twice got lucky
against Australia with last-minute drop goals.

You seemed to know almost to the pint how the England
players celebrated their Ashes victory. What did the team do
after winning the Rugby World Cup in 2003?

 Well, as a *Sun* columnist I am well informed on the gossip
front, and my newspaper colleagues tell me that the
England rugby heroes tried to drink Sydney dry for the two
days before they got on board a British Airways flight
home. They then managed to get through all the alcohol on

YOU CAN'T BEAT A GOOD RUCK 125

the plane before it landed at Heathrow. Mike Tindall went for the David Boon challenge of fifty-four cans of beer. But he made the tactical error of drinking Fosters, which comes in cans twice the size of the stubbies that Boon would have been drinking. He got up to twenty and then passed out. I wonder what his prospective royal ma-in-law thinks of that stat?

 Being serious for a moment, some of the things that go on in the scrums are close to criminal. Those pitbull forwards make Tommy Smith and Norman Hunter seem like pussycats. I remember Kevin Yates becoming the first England player to be charged with biting. It was claimed he tucked into the ear of Simon Fenn after a scrum collapsed in a Premiership match. Fenn lost part of his ear and had to have loads of stitches. I'm just surprised more players are not sent for an early bath.

David Egerton, the former Bath and England number eight, summed up forward play beautifully: 'There is a very simple equation at work here – three good footballers and five complete bastards equal one very useful pack. Of course, if one or two of those bastards can also play some football, you're well on the road to winning every game you play.'

 The rough stuff is nothing new. All Black Cyril Brownlie was the first player sent off in an international against England at Twickenham back in 1925. Players were fighting from the first kick and the referee gave three warnings to the battling forwards before giving Brownlie his marching orders in the ninth minute for stamping on an English player. Brownlie had two brothers who also played for New Zealand in the days when they were known as The Invincibles because they beat everybody in sight.

Rugby is a religion in New Zealand and it's also massive in South Africa, as I discovered when I was playing football and coaching down there. That was the winter sport that got the main media coverage, and of course back then in the early 1970s it was almost exclusively the white man's sport. I remember the All Blacks toured in 1970, on the understanding that their Maori players were given the status of 'honorary whites'.

Willie John McBride led a Lions tour there in 1974 when they won the Test series 3-0. It was reckoned to be the most viciously fought series in the history of rugby. The Lions management had decided the Springboks liked to physically intimidate their opponents with bullyboy tactics, so their plan was to 'get their retaliation in first'.

Willie John later recalled: 'Whenever the Springboks started any rough stuff, we had what we called a code-ninety-nine. As soon as I shouted ninety-nine, that was the signal for all Lions players to launch an attack on their nearest South African opponent. Our thinking was that the referee would not see everything, and he would not be silly enough to send us all off.

'In what became known as "the Battle of Boet Erasmus Stadium", JPR Williams – on hearing the ninety-nine call – famously ran half the length of the pitch to launch himself at the player we called Moaner, Johannes van Heerden. He flattened him with a punch that the referee didn't see because he was too busy trying to separate us warring forwards.'

There was a sequel. JPR revealed recently that he had been on a train travelling to Cardiff when a huge South African stood over him and said: 'You don't recognise me, do you?' JPR said no, and then the South African introduced himself as Johannes 'Moaner' van Heerden! JPR prepared himself for some sort of retaliation, and said: 'He sat alongside me and we talked rugby for the rest of the journey without him once mentioning how I had punched him. He was a proper gentleman.'

 Rugby players are a breed apart. JPR was as hard as any of the pitbull forwards you were talking about. Playing for Bridgend against the All Blacks in 1978, he was caught at the bottom of a ruck, and John Ashworth raked him, tearing a huge hole in his cheek. JPR lost two pints of blood and had to get thirty stitches . . . and then played on after treatment! JPR's dad was making the main speech at the after-match dinner, and when he mentioned the raking incident ten of the All Blacks got up and walked out.

 It has to be said that the Aussies are as vicious with their sledging in rugby as in cricket. David Campese, probably the greatest wing ever to play the game, spent his career winding up the opposition, and the English in particular. He said Will Carling had the finesse of a castrated bull, and that England had set the game back fifty years with their boring style of play. I wonder which goon at the BBC decided it was a good idea to ask Campo to present England with the Team of the Year award in 2003. Clive Woodward described it as 'crass' and 'a bad error of judgement'. On another occasion, Aussie coach Bob Dwyer said Campo had a loose wire between his brain and his mouth.

 Will Carling wasn't backward in coming forward with a strong opinion. I thought it was one of the sporting quotes of the twentieth century when in 1995 he described the members of the Rugby Football Union's committee as 'fifty-seven old farts'. It was an accusation that could equally have been aimed at the Football Association. The Establishment hit back childishly by stripping Carling of his England captaincy, but the other players stood firm behind their captain and when the RFU approached senior England players to take over, they were rejected. Player power won the day and Carling was reinstated.

There was a great team spirit in the England camp when Will was captain, and he was prepared to join in the fun. He could not be missed as he sat at the team lunch table during a training get-together with the international squad. A snooker cue had been pushed through the sleeves of his jacket, and he looked like an umpire signalling a wide. The entire team then watched him try to sup his soup of the day. This was Will's punishment for being voted the worst performer in that morning's training session. All great for the team spirit.

 I loved the true story about ex-London Irish captain Gary Halpin, who suddenly upped and walked away from a scrum during a club match. He left the pitch and was gone for five minutes. He had heard the public address announcer reading out the registration of a car that needed to be moved. It belonged to Gary! He said later: 'What annoyed me is that I was obviously not concentrating hard enough on the match, otherwise the message would never have sunk in.'

He was doing the after-dinner circuit you and I have been on and was on his feet talking when a fight broke out at one of the tables. Gary paused in mid speech and said: 'I'll have a fiver on the guy in the blue suit!' The two main protagonists and the rest of the guests fell about laughing and that was the end of the trouble.

Another London Irish anecdote. Aidan Higgins, who weighed in at around twenty stones, could not squeeze into his number five shirt before a match against Leicester, so he borrowed the number twenty-one shirt from the substitute prop. As he ran on to the field the Leicester announcer said: 'Ladies and gentlemen, today the London Irish second rower Aidan Higgins will wear the number twenty-one shirt as he cannot fit into the number five shirt.' The other players nearly burst their shirts laughing.

Wales once 'lost' a player in action. They were playing England in Bristol in 1908 when a blanket of fog dropped on the ground. The referee abandoned the match, and the players returned to their dressing rooms. Wales suddenly realised they were a player missing, and they sent out a search party. Fullback Bert Winfield was found patrolling in front of his posts, believing his team were attacking in the England half!

Gareth Edwards listened with a straight face as Welsh team coach John Dawes outlined his plan to introduce codewords at a training session before a match against England.

'When you want the open-side flanker to make a break, the codeword should start with a "P",' said Dawes. 'If you want a break on the blind side, use a codeword beginning with "S".'

He tossed the ball to master scrum-half Edwards, who put it into the scrum and shouted the codeword: 'Psychology!'

There are scores of tales about Gareth the Joker. I heard a lot of them when I went to his sixtieth birthday dinner at the Celtic Manor Resort in the summer of 2007. Playing for the British Lions

Gareth Edwards, Welsh scrum-half legend who took the P (PA Photos).

against the Springboks on the 1971 tour, Gareth was stamped on by the giant South African forward Frik du Preez.

The Cardiff man was at the bottom of a ruck, and the referee penalised him rather than the player raking his studs across his leg.

Gareth let fly with a verbal volley and the referee blew his whistle and stopped the game. He summoned Lions skipper Tom Kiernan and complained: 'This player just swore at me, captain.'

Kiernan looked towards Edwards, who threw his arms wide in a gesture of innocence. 'What, me, ref?' he said. 'I wasn't swearing. I was talking in Welsh.'

Irishman Kiernan nodded his head. 'To be sure, that's what he was doing, referee,' he said. 'He is always jabbering away in Welsh. Perhaps to your ears it sounds like swearing. It's a rough-sounding language, so it is.'

The referee rather reluctantly accepted Kiernan's explanation. 'In that case,' he said to Gareth, 'I owe you an apology.'

Kiernan later asked Gareth: 'Did you swear at the ref?'

Edwards shrugged his shoulders. 'I swear I didn't,' he said with a distinct twinkle in his eye. 'Mind you, I might have mispronounced Frik's name.'

Gareth was once tackled by England three-quarter John Spencer, who could match him as a joker. As they became tangled up in a loose maul, Spencer clung to Edwards and chanted in his ear: 'I'm not a pheasant plucker, I'm a pheasant plucker's son . . . When I'm not plucking pheasants . . .' It was a verse that John had taught Gareth at their last social meeting.

 Former England wing David Duckham, a good pal of mine, was also at that Gareth Edwards birthday bash. He was known throughout Welsh rugby as Dai Duckham, because they paid him the compliment of saying he played rugby like a Welshman. His special memory of Edwards: 'Gareth and I both had the superstition of wanting to run on to the pitch last. We ran side by side from the dressing-room area for an international at Cardiff Arms Park. I didn't dare look at him because I knew he would make me laugh. As we reached the pitch he stepped right in front of me, rolled up his jersey and revealed the reserve match ball. "Here, have a look at this, Dai," he said. "It's the only time you'll see it this afternoon."'

 The king of the raconteurs had to be Dr A. J. (Tony) O'Reilly, the pin-up boy of Irish rugby who became the billionaire boss of Heinz. He had hundreds of stories to tell, and this was just one of them: 'I was playing in a match for Leinster when I put my shoulder out. Just a minor dislocation, you know.

The physio was summoned and as he put a firm grip on my shoulder and pushed hard I could not help but let out a yell.

'The physio, a local GP, said: "Come on, O'Reilly, I've just delivered a baby and the mother didn't make half as much fuss."

'"Maybe not," I said. "But you weren't trying to push it back in."'

O'Reilly was playing in a match for Ireland against England at Twickenham during which Phil Horrocks-Taylor cleverly dummied his way past Irish stand-off Mick English to score a try. 'Horrocks went this way,' said O'Reilly, 'Taylor went that way, and poor Mick was left holding the hyphen.'

When O'Reilly was recalled for his final Ireland rugby international cap against England at the age of thirty-four in 1971, he arrived at Twickenham in a chauffeur-driven Rolls. Skipper Willie-John McBride took him on one side and said: 'Tony, you won't mind me saying to your face that you're no longer in your prime. The tactic I suggest you adopt is save your energy and just shake your jowls at your opposite number.'

 I used to drag on the odd cigarette during my playing days, and had several happy years puffing a pipe. But I was a novice smoker compared with the exceptional French fullback Serge Blanco. He used to get through sixty cigarettes a day when he was at his peak. Amazingly, he kicked the smoking habit virtually the same time as he finished playing. Like Tony O'Reilly, he is now a billionaire, with a string of clothing stores, three hotels and is the leading executive of French rugby. What a player! I once saw him collect the ball behind the French posts and engineer a try against England in a move that swept the length of the pitch, with him involved all the way.

There was a time many years ago, Greavsie, when you could drink a bit, but you would not have kept pace with giant French second-row forward Lucien Mias. On the eve of an international match against South Africa he downed a bottle of brandy, and played through the fog of a hangover. Witnesses described his performance as the greatest individual forward display ever seen as France powered to victory. He was a GP, nicknamed Dr Pack. He claimed he used alcohol as medication.

That great West Country character Gareth Chilcott could also knock 'em back. Following his last appearance, he announced: 'I'm now going for a quiet pint, followed by fifteen noisy ones.'

Mick Skinner was another unforgettable character. We were fellow columnists on the *Sun*, when he was nicknamed Mick the Munch because of his biting tackles. The larger-than-life Geordie made his reputation with a crunching tackle against giant six-foot-four-inch French captain Marc Cecillon in the 1991 World Cup quarter-final in Paris. He not only stopped man mountain Cecillon in his tracks but then drove him back five yards. It became known in rugby folklore as *Le Tackle*. Asked about how he virtually picked Cecillon up while pushing him back, Mick – the waistcoated one – said: 'My adrenalin took over, and it was if I was moving one of the French Alps.'

I was told a Mickey Skinner story of how he once refused to sign a young boy's autograph after the lad had politely asked: 'Please, Mr Skinner, could I have your autograph?'

Mick said sharply, 'No! Not until you ask me properly.'

'Please, sir, can I have your autograph?' the boy said, suddenly sounding like Oliver asking for more.

Mick 'The Munch' Skinner on the
rampage for England
(S&G/PA Photos).

'No!' Skinner snapped again. Just as the boy's father was
preparing to give him a piece of his mind, Mick added: 'You will
only get my autograph if you say: "Oi, Fat One, give me your
autograph."'

The boy falteringly said: 'Oi, Fat One, give me your autograph.'

Mick duly signed, tousled the boy's hair and sent him and his
father happily on their way.

 Pierre Danos, French scrum-half, was knocked out during
a violent match against Northern Transvaal in Pretoria in
1958. Two ambulancemen tried to put the protesting Danos
on a stretcher. French prop forward Alfred 'The Rock'

Roques intervened on behalf of the groggy Danos, and flattened one of the stretcher-bearers with a mighty right uppercut. They used the stretcher to carry off the ambulanceman.

Bob Hiller, a fullback famed for his kicking accuracy, was taking his time preparing for a crucial kick for the British Lions during a tour of New Zealand. As he dug at the turf to build himself a mound on which to rest the ball, a home spectator shouted: 'Do you want a shovel, Hiller?' Bob paused, looked in the direction of the spectator and shouted back in his best Oxford University tones: 'No, your mouth will do, old chap!' He then proceeded to kick the ball between the posts before turning back to his heckler and delivering a double Harvey Smith signal.

Hiller and JPR Williams were drafted in as makeshift forwards during a training session that same 1971 Lions tour of New Zealand. They packed down against Scotland's dynamic prop forward Ian 'Mighty Mouse' McLauchlan, a notorious prankster. As the ball was fed into the scrum Hiller suddenly gave out a yelp and jumped up holding his ear where McLauchlan had taken a nibble. JPR was heard to mutter: 'He'd better not try that on me.'

Mighty Mouse either didn't hear or didn't heed the warning. During the next scrumdown he fastened his teeth on JPR's ear, and the next thing he knew he was lying flat on his back. JPR had reacted to the bite with a swinging right to the jaw. 'That,' said JPR to the amusement of everybody but the dazed McLauchlan, 'proves that my bark is worse than your bite.'

New Zealand rugby coach Eric Watson introduced an unusual training method for the 1980 All Blacks tourists.

He was so concerned at how many passes were going astray that he made the three-quarters practise their passing movements while using a house brick instead of a ball. The press dubbed them the 'All Bricks'.

It was the final after-match banquet of a Scotland rugby tour of Argentina that had been scarred by brawls and stiff-armed tackles, with the Argentinians as the main perpetrators. Jim Telfer, Scotland's captain and noted for his forthright views, stood and made a brief but no-punches-pulled speech.

'If you wish to be accepted internationally you must cut out the dirty play,' he said. 'In all my time in the game I have never come up against opposition so set on intimidatory tactics.'

Jim sat down and let the interpreter translate his tough words into Spanish. The interpretation took just twenty seconds.

When the interpreter sat down, Jim asked him what he had said. He replied: 'I thought it best just to use that bit about what a beautiful country this is. I did not wish to cause an international incident.'

Another interpreter story, this time involving your great fullback Gavin Hastings. He skippered the Scottish side that won in France for the first time in thirty years in 1995. At the post-match banquet he used bilingual second row forward Damian Cronin as his translator. Gavin profusely thanked the French for their warm hospitality, for taking defeat so well, and talked about their good sportsmanship and their great flair for rugby. He thought he had given a good speech, but not one to justify the standing ovation. It was some time later that he discovered that Cronin had finished off his translation with the words: 'Thank you so much for listening to my speech. I am now going upstairs to my hotel bedroom to make mad, passionate love to my wife!'

 Paul Burke was lining up a crucial conversion kick for Cardiff against Newport at the Arms Park when a drunken spectator ran on to the pitch and kicked the ball into the stands. Burke recovered the ball, waited for the invader to be frogmarched away by police and then coolly kicked the last-minute conversion to clinch victory. The Irish international later said: 'I prefer not to comment on the incident. I subscribe to the theory that it's better to keep your mouth shut and appear stupid rather than to open it and remove all doubt.'

 Let's finish our dip into the world of rugby, Saint, with another tale from that master Irish storyteller Tony O'Reilly, whose career with Ireland was one long sporting laugh. He gave this lovely taste of the build-up to an England–Ireland match at Twickenham in the 1950s:

'We were always devising plans to reduce England's home advantage at Twickenham. One I remember was sending a misshapen Irish forward with a rugby ball stuck up the back of his jersey to make him look like Quasimodo, into the England dressing room.

'We timed it so that he arrived at what we knew would be the peak moment of a call to arms by their skipper Eric Evans.

'Just as Eric was giving his final passionate harangue – remember Waterloo (with an Irish-born captain in Wellington, incidentally) and Alamein (with another in Montgomery) – our man pushed open the door and said, "Sorry to be disturbing you, lads, but would any of you be having some hairy twine I could be borrowing for me boots?"

'It didn't help us win the match, but it provided us with a good laugh. And that's surely what sport and life should be all about.'

Saint's Rugby Joke

Martin Johnson is curious to find out how Warren Gatland has turned around the fortunes of the Welsh team so quickly, and he decides to go to Cardiff to see how he coaches his team. He is less than impressed by the training routines, so he asks Gatland how he gets his players so sharp.

'Well, it's simple,' says Gatland. 'It's a method I learned while playing and coaching in my homeland of New Zealand. I keep my players on their toes by asking them a difficult question. This keeps them alert and mentally sharp.'

Martin is fascinated. 'Can you give me an example?' he asks.

Gatland summons skipper Ryan Jones to join them, and asks him: 'He is not your brother, but still he is your father's son. Who is he?'

'That's easy,' Ryan answers immediately. 'Of course, it's me'.

'You see? That's the way you keep them mentally sharp,' Gatland says to Johnson.

Keen to try this with the England players, Johnson decides to test one of his brightest players, Jonny Wilkinson. 'Jonny, see if you can answer this question,' he says. 'He is not your brother, but he is still your father's son, who is he?'

Jonny's forehead suddenly creases with concentration.

'That's a difficult one,' he says. 'Can I sleep on it tonight and tell you in the morning?'

'OK,' says Johnson. 'Call me first thing in the morning.'

'Anyway,' continues Jonny, 'why have you asked me the question?' Johnson explains it has to do with a New Zealand coaching method he has heard about.

That night, unable to answer the question, Jonny has a bright idea and phones Zinzan Brook and asks him for the answer. 'You're from New Zealand, Zinzan,' he says, 'so you're bound to know the answer to this question . . . he is not your brother, but he is still your father's son. Who is he?'

'That's easy, it's me!' says Zinzan.

First thing the next morning Jonny calls Martin Johnson, brimming with confidence.

'So you've worked it out, Jonny,' Martin says.

'Once I started thinking about it,' says Jonny, 'I found it pretty easy. The answer, of course, is Zinzan Brook.'

'Don't be so bloody stupid,' says Johnson. 'It's Ryan Jones.'

Greavsie's Rugby Joke

A rugby referee died and went to heaven. Stopped by St Peter at the gates he was told that only special people who had performed gallant deeds and had the courage of their convictions could enter. If the ref could describe a situation in his life where he had shown these characteristics, he would be allowed in.

'Well,' said the ref, 'I was reffing a Calcutta Cup match between Scotland and England at Murrayfield. Scotland were four points in the lead with a minute to go. The England wing raced down the touchline, and passed inside to his centre. He fed the ball to the lock who was driven on by his forwards. The ball was then picked up by the scrum-half but he dropped the ball as he dived for the line. In my opinion he had been obstructed by the Scotland fullback and I awarded England a penalty try.'

'Yes, that was gallant of you and you had the courage of your convictions,' St Peter said. 'I will, of course, have to check the facts.' He goes to the records office, and returns a moment later. 'I'm very sorry,' he said, 'there is no record of this. Can you help me with the date that this happened?'

The ref looked at his watch and replied, 'Forty-five seconds before I arrived at these gates.'

The Talk of Rugby

John O'Neill, Australian rugby chief executive:

It doesn't matter whether it's cricket, rugby union, rugby league, we all hate England.

Oscar Wilde

Rugby is a good occasion for keeping thirty bullies far from the centre of the city.

Anton Oliver, All Black hooker describing the dressing-room mood after their 2007 World Cup defeat by France:

Sort of desolate, decayed, the smell of – I don't want to dramatise it – but death, you know. That is what it feels like, no-man's-land, and it is not a nice place to be.

Jim Glennon, Irish lock:

I may not have been very tall or very athletic, but the one thing I did have was the most effective backside in world rugby.

Bill Beaumont

Playing in the second row doesn't require a lot of intelligence. You've got to be bloody crazy to play there for a start.

Max Boyce

We were at the cemetery for my uncle's funeral in 1986 when somebody got the score from the Arms Park – Wales 15, France 23. It cast a gloom over the entire proceedings.

Gareth Davies

We've lost seven of our last eight matches. The only team we've beaten is Western Samoa. It's a good job we didn't play the whole of Samoa.

Johan le Roux, after an eighteen-month suspension for biting the ear of All Blacks skipper Sean Fitzgerald:

I feel I probably should have torn it off. Then at least I could say, 'Look, I've returned to South Africa with the guy's ear.'

Paul Randall

I think Brian Moore's gnashers are the kind you get from a DIY shop and hammer in yourself. He is the only player we have who looks like a French forward.

Geoff Cooke, after England had been hammered by the All Blacks in the 1995 World Cup:

I don't know about us not having a Plan B. When things went wrong, we looked like we didn't have a Plan A.

Mike Watkins

I didn't know what was going on at the start in the swirling wind at Lansdowne Road. The flags were all pointing in different directions and I thought the Irish had starched them just to fool us.

Fernandez Lobbe, Argentine forward on the prospect of playing the All Blacks in the 2007 World Cup (they won):

If we have to play against New Zealand, I'll explain it like this. To win, their fifteen players have to have a diarrhoea and we will have to put snipers around the field shooting at them and then we have to play the best match of our lives.

JPR Williams, on a Welsh defeat by Australia in 1984:

No leadership, no ideas. Not even enough imagination to thump someone in the line-out when the ref wasn't looking.

Referee, to Princess Anne's son Peter Phillips as he tossed before a match in which he skippered Gordonstoun:

Grandmother or tails, sir?

Phil Bennett, pre-match pep talk before facing England in 1977 (Wales won 14-9):

Look what these bastards have done to Wales. They've taken our coal, our water, our steel. They buy our houses and they only live in them for a fortnight every twelve months. What have they given us? Absolutely nothing. We've been exploited, raped, controlled and punished by the English – and that's who you're playing this afternoon.

Dudley Wood, former head of the RFU:

The relationship between the Welsh and the English is based on trust and understanding. They don't trust us and we don't understand them.

Mike Gibson

Tony Ward is the most important rugby player in Ireland. His legs are far more important to his country than even those of Marlene Dietrich were to the film industry. A little hairier, maybe, but a pair of absolute winners.

Gavin Hastings, on Jonah Lomu:

There's no doubt about it, he's a big bastard.

Tony O'Reilly, on the legendary All Black known throughout rugby as Pine Tree:

Colin Meads is the kind of player you expect to see emerging from a ruck with the remains of a jockstrap between his teeth.

Ray Gravell

You've got to get your first tackle in early, even if it's late.

Jean-Pierre Rives

The whole point of rugby is that it is, first and foremost, a state of mind, a spirit.

7 THE CUPS THAT CHEER

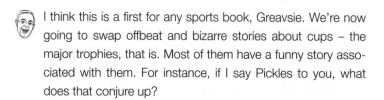

I think this is a first for any sports book, Greavsie. We're now going to swap offbeat and bizarre stories about cups – the major trophies, that is. Most of them have a funny story associated with them. For instance, if I say Pickles to you, what does that conjure up?

Well, I could say, 'What's on the table, Mabel?' and Wilfred Pickles, but that would be a joke lost on anybody under fifty. So I'll give a straight answer and say that was the name of the dog that found the Jules Rimet Trophy.

Correct. Speaking as a Scot who was watching from the sidelines, that had to be one of the funniest incidents in sporting history. 'Only the English', we said, 'could lose the World Cup before a ball had been kicked.'

It might have been funny to you, Saint, but for us English it was a hell of an embarrassment. During the war the trophy was kept in a shoebox under the bed of a French FIFA official rather than risk letting the Nazis take it as part of their plunder. The Nazis couldn't get their hands on it, but a petty criminal in London outwitted the great brains of the Football Association.

They took charge of the trophy in January 1966 – six months before the Wembley final. Within eight weeks they had lost it! The FA loaned it to the Stanley Gibbons stamp company for them to show off in a glass-fronted display cabinet at a public exhibition at Central Hall in Westminster.

Two uniformed officers guarded the trophy, supported by two plainclothes officers during the day. The only time it did not have full guard was on a Sunday, when the Central Hall was used for Methodist services.

 Let me stop you there. You're saying that the trophy was left unattended while the worshippers were in the hall?

 Well, Saint, be fair – you wouldn't expect anybody to steal a trophy during a religious service, would you. On Sunday 20 March the guards did a noon check after the service had finished. They were rather shocked to find that someone had forced open the display case and the trophy plinth was empty.

A massive cup hunt was launched, and a week later to a background of world laughter a chap called David Corbett was taking his dog Pickles for a walk in Upper Norwood when he decided he wanted a piss against a hedge – the dog, that is. As he cocked his leg, Pickles noticed a parcel and started to sniff it. It was wrapped in old newspaper. Mr Corbett picked it up and found, to his astonishment, that he was holding the World Cup . . . four months before Mooro got his hands on it at Wembley.

Pickles and his owners collect the reward for recovering the Jules Rimet trophy after a robbery that drove the Football Association barking mad (PA Photos).

At first Corbett was suspected as an accomplice, but after close questioning he was able to come up with an alibi. He later picked up a reward of £6000. The petty thief got two years inside.

 The Brazilians, who won the trophy outright in 1970, were even more careless than the English and it was stolen in 1983. It has not been seen since and is believed to have been melted down, and to be adorning a hundred fingers in the shape of jewellery.

Right, now it's my turn and I have a story to tell about a prize that is much older than the Jules Rimet Trophy. I am referring to rugby's famous Calcutta Cup.

It is, of course, of Indian workmanship, approximately eighteen inches high, and has a main body that is made of melted-down silver rupees and is finely engraved, with three king cobras forming the handles. The domed lid is surmounted by a carving of an elephant which is, so I am informed, copied from the Viceroy's own stock and is complete with a howdah.

Okay, Saint, I know you've done your homework. What the heck is a howdah when it's at home?

I thought everybody knew that a howdah – or a houdah, depending where you are in India – is the ornate carriage that is positioned on top of an elephant at ceremonial events.

The melted-down rupees were from the subscriptions the soldiers had paid into their Calcutta Rugby Football Club before disbanding because the climate was not conducive to the game.

The inscription at the wooden base of the Cup reads in engraved capital letters 'THE CALCUTTA CUP'. Of course, Calcutta is now known as Kolkata, and is the capital of West Bengal. But when the Cup was first made in the 1870s old Queen Vic was Empress of India, and it was a trophy played for by her loyal English and Scottish soldiers in twenty-a-side rugger matches. They brought the trophy home to the United Kingdom with them in 1878 and presented it to the RFU, on the understanding it would be competed for annually between the English and the Scots.

All very interesting, but where's the funny bit?

Fast forward about 110 years. It's 1988 and a group of drunken Scottish and English international players are on the loose in Edinburgh. They had been celebrating – the Scots – and drowning their sorrows – the English – at the after-match banquet following Scotland's Calcutta Cup victory that afternoon.

The players were sat at tables close to each other, and as boring speech followed boring speech they started to wind each other up. It started with firing bread rolls, and then – as they became more and more puppets of alcohol – they began to try to out-sing each other, with typical bawdy rugby songs that made the blazered Old Farts wriggle uncomfortably in their seats.

Let me quote Scottish forward John Jeffrey. He was prominent in the Affair of the Flying Calcutta Cup and went on record with his story on ITV in the days when our *Saint and Greavsie* show took in all sorts of offbeat items.

The Big Man said: 'My memory is still hazy of what exactly went on that night in Edinburgh. In those days the captain used to take the Calcutta Cup around, filling it with drink and offering it to all and sundry.

'I remember it was full of whisky, and we decided to tip it over the head of that belligerent England hooker Brian Moore. He got a good soaking and started chasing us out of the dining room, looking for revenge.

'So we just ran through the hotel and were suddenly out in the street. We jumped into a taxi, still carrying the Calcutta Cup with us.

'We went into two or three pubs and then came back to the hotel. I have only a hazy memory of what happened after that, but the Cup certainly came back.

'We took it away and it was not damaged and by the time we came back with it the Cup was damaged, so I have to hold my hands up and say, "Yes, I was one of those responsible."

'One thing I would like to correct. Brian Moore put it around that we filled the Cup with champagne. Only poncy Englishmen would do that. We treated it properly by filling it with Scotland's finest malt whisky.'

I think there's a fairly important part missing from John's story, Saint. Didn't he play rugby with the Cup?

 I'm coming to that bit, if you'll stop interrupting. Missing from John's version is the fact that he and England forward Dean Richards . . .

 Police Constable Richards . . .

 Yes, he was in the force at the time and he and John Jeffrey were proceeding in a disorderly manner along Prince's Street. They were passing the Cup back and forth to each other when one of them – neither can remember which it was – dropped the Cup and gave it a severe dent. In fact, somebody said it was no longer the Calcutta Cup, but more the Calcutta Shield.

All hell broke loose when the Cup was returned damaged. The upshot was that John Jeffrey was banned from international rugby for six months, while the Old Farts at Twickenham caused a stink by only giving Richards a one-match suspension. They clearly did not think so highly of the Calcutta Cup.

 I can add a bit more to the story. Brian Moore got hold of a photo showing Jeffrey and Richards throwing the Cup as if it were a rugby ball. Deano was apparently wearing a tea-cosy on his head. A newspaper offered Mooro ten grand for the photo, but he refused because he knew it would have dropped Richards into even deeper trouble. You could say that Mooro wasn't hooked.

In truth, Saint, I don't think it was the real Calcutta Cup. Following the fiasco with the football World Cup, all the major trophies now have replicas that are used for public appearances.

The Calcutta Cup, which featured in a street passing game (S&G/PA Photos).

 You're wrong there. It was THE Calcutta Cup. It only comes out on the day of the match, and it was the real one that was presented that day. Any other time it is one of the replicas that is seen in public. Over to you for some FA Cup stories . . .

 You and I both held the real thing as players at Wembley and on open-top buses the day after winning it, but now when it's paraded it is a replica. The winning captain accepts it, but as soon as they come off the pitch the Cup is swapped and the original put in safe keeping.

It is the oldest football competition in the world, dating back to 1871–72, and there have actually been four FA Cup trophies. The first was famously nicked from a Birmingham shop window while Aston Villa were the holders in 1895. The thieves melted it down to make half crowns.

The second was presented to Lord Kinnaird in 1910 as a mark of his long service as player and FA President.

That trophy was bought by Birmingham City chairman David Gold in a Christie's auction for close to half a million pounds in 2005.

Correct. He saved it for the nation, because there were several overseas bidders. It is now on display at the National Football Museum in Preston.

The FA ordered a new, slightly larger, trophy in 1911. It was designed by Fattorini's of Bradford but didn't travel far in its first year. Bradford City were the winners, the only time a team from Bradford has reached the final.

That's the one you and I held and drank champagne from as winning players, Saint. It still exists but is now too fragile to be used, so an exact replica was made and has been in use since the 1992 final.

The most unbelievable – but true – story about the third FA Cup centres around that old rascal, the much-mourned Peter Osgood.

He was a winner of the trophy with Chelsea and then Southampton. After the banquet in London that followed Southampton's sensational 1976 victory over Man United, the club somehow managed to put the treasured trophy in the keeping of the old King of the King's Road.

He had plenty of partying experience at Chelsea to call on, and was leading the celebrations when suddenly entrusted with the job of making sure the FA Cup got back safely to Southampton. It was like giving the biggest of the nuts the keys to the asylum.

So it was that at three o'clock on the morning after the final a seriously sozzled Ossie was showing off the FA Cup to astonished Saints supporters having a coffee at a mobile snackbar on the A3.

Then, as you do, Ossie took the Cup home and slept with it! 'It was the best way of looking after it and keeping it safe,' Ossie later told me with the sort of logic that made sense only to him. What a lovely character, but he could be as daft as Gazza's brush.

 Now for the trophy I would most like to get my hands on, the old Claret Jug awarded to winners of the Open since way back in 1872. It was originally known as the Golf Champion Trophy, and was crafted from solid silver by Mackay Cunningham of Edinburgh. The first Open Champion to receive the new trophy was the 1873 winner, Tom Kidd, but Tom Morris Junior's name was the first to be engraved on it as the 1872 winner.

The prize when the Open was first launched in 1860 was the Challenge Belt, made of rich Morocco leather, embellished with a silver buckle and emblems. The Jug was ordered after Tom Morris Junior won the belt outright with three successive victories.

It is now, of course, a replica trophy that is presented to Open winners. The Golf Champion Trophy is on permanent display in The Royal and Ancient Golf Clubhouse. It sits alongside the original first prize, the Challenge Belt, which was donated to the club in 1908 by the grandchildren of Tom Morris Senior.

 Trust the Jocks to come up with a trophy linked to drink. I'm just surprised it wasn't a whisky decanter.

 Royal and Ancient Club officials were in need of a stiff drink in 1982 when they realised they had presented champion Tom

Watson with the original, priceless Claret Jug by mistake. So what happens?

Watson thought he had the usual replica and was fairly casual about it when he took it home. He later confessed: 'I was making a golf swing with a number two iron in the house one day, clattered the trophy, and it fell to the floor. The fall bent the throat of the jug. We have a silversmith in Kansas City, but I wanted to see if I could do something with it myself. I took the trophy downstairs, got some felt and a pair of vice grips, and bent the silver back in place. It didn't crimp or crease. Nobody knew the difference. I had no idea it was the original, and I wondered why it was so fragile. The Open officials couldn't wait to get their hands on it when I returned it the following year. I don't think it's been allowed in anybody's hands since.'

 Tom Lehman's daughters were playing with it at their home after his victory in 1996, using it as a doll. They threw it around so much that they bent the jug and Tom had to take it to a repairers to get it straightened out before he could return it.

 Even worse, Lehman took the trophy to a charity dinner in Minneapolis. He put it in the care of Alissa Herron, sister of tour professional Tim. Alissa and some friends decided to take the treasured trophy on a midnight pub crawl, showing it off to impressed late-night drinkers. A suspicious bartender recognised the Jug, and telephoned the police to say it had been stolen. Police were ready to launch a hunt until Lehman assured them it was in safe hands.

 They could have put Alissa in the jug.

The Ryder Cup was damaged during the riotous celebrations by the European team in 1997 and had to be taken to a Birmingham jeweller's to be repaired after it had been dented and its base virtually torn off. Nobody owned up to causing the damage . . . not that any of them would have been able to remember!

Few trophies can match the adventures of ice hockey's famous Stanley Cup. When first donated in 1892 by Englishman Lord Stanley, Governor General of Canada, it was a silver bowl that was just eight inches high and twelve inches across. So many banded bases have since been added to take in the inscriptions of winners that it now stands three feet high and weighs thirty-six pounds.

It has been dropped to the bottom of a swimming pool, left on a roadside embankment, stolen and returned, used as a flowerpot by a housewife who discovered it abandoned, has been urinated in, used as a baptismal font, been drop-kicked on to a frozen canal by a drunken player, has shared the bed of a hockey player and his wife, and was once used to feed oats to a Kentucky Derby winner. Nowadays the Hockey Hall of Fame employs a full-time security guard whenever it leaves its exhibition cabinet.

There's an even older sports trophy than the Claret Jug – the America's Cup, which was first competed for in 1851. The trophy, an ornate silver-plated ewer designed and crafted in 1848, was donated to the Royal Yacht Squadron by Sir Henry Paget. Fifteen British-based yachts entered the first race in 1851, and one from the United States. It was a yacht-schooner called *America*, and it won the race round the Isle of Wight by twenty minutes. When Queen Victoria asked: 'Who was second?' the answer came, 'There is no second, your Majesty.'

The trophy became a challenge trophy, displayed at the

New York Yacht Club and named the America's Cup after the first winner.

Of all the trophies we've discussed, it's the only one that has survived a sledgehammer attack. A nutter tried to smash it when it was on display in New Zealand after the Kiwis had won the trophy in 1997. The damage was so severe that it was feared the cup was beyond repair. Garrard's, the London silversmiths who had first manufactured it, restored the trophy to its original condition, free of charge. We might not be able to win it, Saint, but we know how to keep it shipshape.

 It was just as well that Liverpool got to keep the Champions League trophy for good after they won it in that fantastic

Liverpool skipper Steve Gerrard kisses the Champions League trophy before it took a battering (Dusan Vranic/PA Photos).

2005 final in Istanbul. When the Reds came back from 3-0 down to beat AC Milan on penalties, it was the fifth time they had won the trophy. During the after-match celebrations it got dented when striker Milan Baros dropped it at the team's hotel.

The Cup is now on show at the Anfield museum with the dent still visible. It was decided not to repair it because it was felt it gave the trophy character.

 One last story, and it centres on the holy grail of American Football, the Super Bowl. It's just a baby compared with most of the trophies we have discussed, but it rates highest of all the prizes in American sport.

The trophy was born in 1966, when a Tiffany design chief was seated at a luncheon next to National Football League commissioner Pete Rozelle who wanted a cup for a national competition. The designer sketched a tilted football on a table napkin, and the Super Bowl instantly had an image.

Tiffany's have designed a new one every year since then, and it is kept by the winning NFL team.

The Super Bowl was renamed the Vince Lombardi Trophy in 1970, in tribute to the legendary Green Bay Packers coach, whose team won the first two Super Bowl finals.

 Bill Shankly modelled himself on Lombardi. As you'll see from the Lombardi quotes we list at the end of this chapter, you could be listening to Shanks talking.

 There was a panic in 1991 when the New York Giants thought they'd lost the Super Bowl within two hours of collecting it. Just as a search was being organised for a possible thief, an NFL executive found it lying under the wreckage of empty champagne bottles and broken glasses in the locker room.

I think our cup has just about overfloweth, Saint.

Saint's Cup Jokes

A Newcastle fan in black and white striped shirt sits on a London-bound train, on his way to Wembley to see United in the FA Cup final. In a cage he carries a good luck magpie.

Sitting opposite him is a Sunderland supporter, who leans forward and says: 'They'll never let you into the new Wembley Stadium with that pig.'

The Newcastle fan says: 'Don't be so stupid, man. This isn't a pig. This is the club mascot, a magpie.'

'I was talking to the magpie,' says the Sunderland man.

* * *

Prime Minister Gordon Brown wrote to John Terry after his missed penalty had cost Chelsea the European Champions League Cup. Unfortunately, Mr Brown's letter missed the post.

Greavsie's Cup Jokes

Tiger Woods reports for his Ryder Cup practice round accompanied by a mongrel dog. A posse of photographers and reporters follow Tiger and the dog down the fairway. He reaches the green in two and sinks a twenty-yard putt for a birdie.

The dog starts to bark and stands on two legs, clapping his front paws together in mimed applause.

'Wow, Tiger, that's some dog you've got there,' one of the reporters says. 'What does he do if you miss a putt?'

'Somersaults,' says Tiger.

'Somersaults?!' repeats the reporter 'That's incredible. How many somersaults does he do?'

'Hmmm,' says Tiger. 'Depends on how hard I kick his ass.'

* * *

The Australian rugby coach takes his squad out for training before a World Cup match against England. 'Okay, guys,' he shouts. 'Take up your usual positions.'

So they all go and stand just in front of the goalposts and wait for the drop-kick to go over.

Vince Lombardi's Talk of Sport

Confidence is contagious. So is lack of confidence.

Fatigue makes cowards of us all.

Football is like life – it requires perseverance, self-denial, hard work, sacrifice, dedication and respect for authority.

I firmly believe that any man's finest hour, the greatest fulfilment of all that he holds dear, is that moment when he has worked his heart out in a good cause and lies exhausted on the field of battle – victorious.

If it doesn't matter who wins or loses, then why do they bother to keep score?

If you are not fired with enthusiasm, take it from me you *will* be fired with enthusiasm.

It's not whether you get knocked down, it's whether you get up.

Once you learn to quit, it becomes a habit.

It's misleading to say that practice makes perfect. Only perfect practice makes perfect.

Show me a good loser, and I'll show you a loser.

Some of us will do our jobs well and some will not, but we will be judged by only one thing – the result.

Teamwork is what the Green Bay Packers were all about. They didn't do it for individual glory. They did it because they loved one another.

The difference between a successful person and others is not a lack of strength, not a lack of knowledge, but rather a lack of will.

The measure of who we are is what we do with what we have.

The only place success comes before work is in the dictionary.

Winning isn't everything, it's the only thing.

8 IT'S A REFFING JOKE

 We now come to our favourite old friends, Greavsie – referees. Don't you just love 'em!

 These days, Saint, to be honest, I feel sorry for them, particularly in football. They have an impossible job in the Premier League, for instance, trying to control a bunch of young, spoilt millionaires. It's easy to knock the refs but I wouldn't do their job for all the loose change in Wayne Rooney's pocket.

 We're not only going to look at football referees for our laughs. Cricket and tennis umpires, rugby refs and touchline judges are also going to be in the firing line.

I loved the humour of former Llanelli forward Doug Perkins, who after his retirement was far-sighted enough to make a fortune as co-founder with his wife of Specsavers. In 2002, as part of a £1-million sponsorship deal, they offered free eye tests to Welsh rugby union referees. To really rub it in, Specsavers were advertised on the shirts of referees for four years.

Then there was the rugby league referee Ronnie Campbell,

who sent Big Jim Mills for an early bath while he was playing for Widnes at Leeds. Jim, a notoriously hard man even by rugby league standards, had a parting shot for the ref as he started the walk back to the dressing rooms: 'Have you got any idea of the bus timetables back to Widnes?' Referee Campbell had been given a lift to the ground by Mills.

 Wigan second-row forward Bill Ashurst couldn't believe it when the referee sent him off for an alleged stiff arm tackle that laid out Leigh's teak-tough Stan Owen. 'But that's only my first offence,' Ashurst protested.

The referee replied: 'I know, it's for your own good 'cos when he comes round he'll kill you.'

Rugby players have a completely different relationship with referees to footballers. They're taught from a young age to have respect for the ref, and I love it when an eighteen-stone second-row forward meekly takes his verbal rollocking from the referee after chinning a king-sized opponent.

During his playing days before he became the big boss, England captain Martin Johnson was heard to ask top referee Steve Lander: 'Is that a new law, ref?' after a penalty decision against him.

Lander was picked up on his microphone replying: 'Jono, if you'll give up trying to referee this match, I will abandon my ambition to be a second-row forward.' What made it even funnier is that Lander was dwarfed by the giant figure of Johnson, who could have stepped off the set of *The Munsters*.

Lawrence Dallaglio was never short of words of advice for the referee. The England and Wasps back-row forward once tried to encourage referee Tony Spreadbury to issue some yellow cards after an eruption of violence from the opposition. The ref responded: 'Lawrence, if you want cards, WH Smith's is a short walk away down the road. I promise we won't miss you.'

An international referee told Ireland's legendary hooker Keith Wood that he was boring his opposite number. His response: 'And you're not too interesting yourself, ref.'

I wonder what the rugby establishment thought when Jonathan Davies, who had vast experience in both rugby union and rugby league, said on television: 'I think you enjoy the game more if you don't know the rules. The good thing is that it puts you on the same wavelength as the referees.'

I've learned the hard way to be careful what I say about referees on the box. Remember me getting sued in our *Saint and Greavsie* show days? I said during a live broadcast that the referee had sent off the player in a League match to get himself into history before his retirement. The referee hit me with a writ for slander, and I was forced to apologise in the High Court for my loose remark. I had to pick up the ref's legal bill and also make a payment to the Referees' Association Benevolent Fund.

So you can understand why I don't put a name to the referee who got involved in a slanging match with an international player, who questioned his parentage. The ref replied: 'I not only knew my father but he taught me how to deal with retards like you. Off!'

There was a very approachable, good-humoured referee when we were playing called Jim Finney.

He had the balls to abandon an international match between Scotland and Austria in 1963 after seventy-nine minutes of mayhem. I was nursing an injury and watched the game from the bench. I have never seen such wicked tackling, mostly from the Austrians but some of our players were guilty of retaliating. We were leading 4-1 and Jim had sent off two Austrians, and could easily have ordered off six other players. Finally, he blew the whistle and waved the game off. 'I was worried somebody was going to get killed,' Finney said later. 'It was like the Third World War out there.'

Jim was one of our finest ever referees. He once told me about another rough match that he handled, the 1966 World Cup quarter-final between West Germany and Uruguay at Hillsborough. He sent off two Uruguayan hatchet men, and said that as he came off at the end of the match and was into the players' tunnel, he got kicked up the arse by Julio Cortes, who was booted out of football for a year. Referees everywhere thought he got off lightly, and should have been banned for life. Say what you like about referees, but once you allow players to lay a finger on them the game will quickly plunge into anarchy.

Jim refereed the 1962 FA Cup final, when we – Tottenham, that is – beat Burnley 3-1. My centre-forward partner Bobby Smith was flagged offside, and said: 'That was a terrible decision, ref!' Jim ignored it, and about ten minutes later Smithy sliced a shot well wide. 'That was a terrible shot, Smithy!' Jim shouted.

He was always firm but fair, and at the end of the final our skipper Danny Blanchflower presented him with the match ball. Of course, Danny being Danny, he couldn't resist a crack. 'Your indecision today, Jim,' he said, 'was final.'

Jim Finney was also in charge of our unforgettable match against our arch rivals Leeds at Anfield in 1967. We, Liverpool,

Referee Jim Finney with Spurs skipper Danny Blanchflower and Burnley captain Jimmy Adamson before the 1962 FA Cup final (PA Photos).

of course, were leading 1-0 through a Roger Hunt goal, and there were just a few minutes to half-time when Leeds goalkeeper Gary Sprake, unchallenged, gathered a harmless through ball.

This was at the Kop end, and our fans groaned because a promising attack had fizzled out to nothing. A groan from the packed Kop – twenty-five thousand squashed together sweating, singing and shouting – sounded like a rumble of angry thunder.

Suddenly the groans gave way to roars of disbelief followed by helpless laughter. The accident-prone Sprake in a Mr Bean moment had managed to throw the ball over his shoulder and into the corner of his own net.

It was as if the Kop choir had decided as one man to pray.

They were literally brought to their knees, almost crying with laughter and unable to cheer a goal that had put us completely in charge of the vital First Division game.

The knots of Leeds fans scattered around the ground were stunned into gaping silence. They were trying to believe the evidence of their own eyes.

All the Leeds players had been running away from Sprake as he went to throw the ball out, and they looked round when they heard the roars. Leeds centre-half Jack Charlton said to referee Finney: 'What the flaming hell's happened?' Or words to that effect.

Finney, one of those lovely old-fashioned referees who used to have a chat and a chuckle with the players and treat them like adults, said: 'Well, Jack, your goalkeeper has just thrown the ball into his net, and I am awarding Liverpool a goal.'

It has gone into the mists of football myth that the Liverpool fans immediately broke into a chorus of 'Careless Hands', the Des O'Connor song that was top of the pops at the time. That's not true, because our supporters were too busy laughing to be able to sing.

No, poor old Gary had to wait until he ran out for the second half to be greeted by the Kop choir in full voice singing 'Careless Hands', geed up by the club disc jockey who played it over the Tannoy.

From that day on Sprake was always welcomed by the song whenever he played at Anfield. He took it well, and rose above the king-size blunder to win thirty-seven Welsh international caps and a stack of medals with Don Revie's Leeds.

 Denis Howell, the former Minister for Sport who was a top-rate ref, was full of anecdotes about his refereeing experiences. The following story captures what soccer was like in the United States when they were first trying to get it launched in a big way:

'It was 1960 and the Americans were making their first all-out attempt to sell soccer to the masses in the United States. They promoted a major competition involving the sixteen clubs that had won their respective League championships around the world.

'I was given the job of refereeing the first match, and before the kick-off I was approached by a television commentator, who clearly had no idea of the laws of the game. "Referee Howell," he said, "can you assist me by telling me what fouls you will be giving?"

'I looked at him with raised eyebrows. "That will be a little difficult because I will be out on the pitch refereeing at the time," I replied, wondering to myself just what sort of service the television viewers were going to be given.

'"No problem," said the commentator's companion, who turned out to be the director. "We have a telephone at the side of the pitch. All we want you to do is pick it up when a goal is scored and just give our commentator a brief description of the play and the name of the players who provide the assists."

'I told them as politely as possible that, to use an Americanism, they could count me out.

'"Okay," said the director. "You're in charge. Now what are we going to do about the commercial breaks?"

'"What do you mean exactly?" I asked, dreading the reply.

'"We'll need you to cause some stoppages so we can fit our advertisements in," the director explained. "Just delay the action a little-biddy bit when the ball is out of play. If a player is injured see to it that he has extended treatment time until we signal to you that we're back covering the match."

'"Sorry," I told him, "but I will have to referee the match in accordance with the rules of FIFA and not for the convenience of television."

'The match announcer then came on the scene, and he asked me to explain how he would know what fouls I was giving. I gave him a crash course in signals so that he would know the difference between a direct and indirect free kick, but I sensed that I was wasting my time.

'When I whistled for the first foul of the match at about the halfway line I was astonished to hear this announcement over the loudspeaker: "Referee Howell has given a foul for handball from which a goal can be scored direct."

'I became very deliberate with my signals for the benefit of the announcer, and when I held up my hand to indicate an indirect free kick following an obstruction, he told the spectators: "Referee Howell has given a free kick for obstruction. This is an indirect free kick, and so no goal can be scored."

'The match was between Paris St Germain and Bayern Munich, and I had my hands full sorting out the language difficulties, although making the Americans understand me was much harder. As Bernard Shaw said, the Americans and English are nations divided by a single language.

'The game had been in progress for about twenty minutes when there was a skirmish involving three or four players. I dived in to separate them and to restore order.

'You can imagine my reaction when the match announcer revealed to one and all: "Referee Howell has given a foul for pushing, tripping, handball and ungentlemanly conduct and a goal can be scored."

'It was at this point that I gave up, and so did the announcer!'

Bob Paisley once told me an unbelievable story of a match in which he played when you and I were just falling in love with the game. 'Liverpool were playing Huddersfield in a League match in the late 1940s,' he said. 'Those were the days when the referee used to leave the match ball on the centre-spot at half-time because spectators knew their place and would not dare put a foot on the sacred turf.

'We came out and lined up for the start of the second half and it was Huddersfield to kick off. I can see it now as clearly as if it were yesterday – the great Peter Doherty, wearing the number ten shirt for Huddersfield, jogging up and down in anticipation as he waited for his centre-forward to tap the ball to him.

'The whistle blew and off we went. Peter was quickly away on one of his magical weaving runs through our defence when suddenly the whistle went again for no apparent reason. We looked up in bewilderment to see the ref and his two linesmen approaching the pitch from the players' tunnel.

'The ref was blowing an Eddie Calvert trumpet solo on his whistle to get us to stop the game so that he could get on. We had started the game without him thanks to a joker in the crowd who had a whistle with him!'

 It was Bobby Moore who used to tell this true, hair-raising story: 'West Ham were playing at Newcastle on a very windy day. In fact I can never remember playing at St James' when it wasn't windy. Anyway, on this particular day I was summoned to the centre-circle for the coin-tossing ritual by referee Ricky Nicholson, who had a striking head of shining black hair. I lost the toss and we had to play into the teeth of the vicious wind. Newcastle quickly had us under pressure and forced an early corner. The referee came and took a position just a few feet from me. I looked at him and then gave a classic double take. He was as bald as a billiard ball. I was fighting to keep a straight face, and he knew it. He gave a dry smile and said quietly, "It's okay, Bob. It's in my pocket. I washed it last night and don't want it blowing off and getting dirty!"

'Of course, the Geordie crowd spotted it and every time he gave a decision against them they chanted, "Keep your hair on." The newspapers the next day had headlines like "Thatch of the Day" and "West Ham Get A Wigging".'

Ricky Nicholson was a real character, a wealthy businessman who used to drive himself to matches in his Rolls Royce. He once booked five Sunderland players when they were playing at St Andrews. When it was time to drive home from Birmingham, he found his car blocked in by the Sunderland team coach.

He went into the dressing room and asked: 'Is your coach driver here?' Bob Stokoe, then Sunderland manager, said, 'F*** me, you're not going to book him as well?'

Ever wondered when the first chant of 'Who's the bastard in the black?' was heard? I can be specific with the answer. It was back in the early days of the game when a prominent referee rejoiced in the name of Segal Richard Bastard. He had played for England before switching to refereeing, and almost caused a riot in the 1878 FA Cup final when he turned down a goal for offside.

The lovely old Toothless Tiger Nobby Stiles, who often autographed our shins in our playing days, was in trouble with referee Pat Partridge when Man United were playing Burnley in a floodlit match at Old Trafford. Nobby kept snapping away at the heels of Burnley centre-forward

Referee Pat Partridge appears to be threatening a bunch of fives, but is actually miming with his whistle to show that he's in charge (Peter Robinson/PA Photos).

Andy Lochhead, and was twice quietly warned to 'watch it' by the ref.

Partridge, good enough to referee in the 1978 World Cup finals, finally lost his patience with Our Nobby, and got his book out in the second half after Nobby's badly timed tackle had sent Lochhead tumbling.

'But it's the floodlights, ref!' Nobby protested. 'They shine in my contact lenses and I can't see a bloody thing.'

Mr Partridge was unimpressed and started to write Nobby's name in his book, misspelling it Styles.

Nobby peered over his shoulder and said: 'You can't even get my bloody name right.'

Partridge countered: 'I'm surprised you can read with the floodlights shining on your contact lenses.'

Nobby gave a toothless grin. 'Nice one, ref,' he said. 'Spell it how you like.'

Arthur Ellis, of *It's A Knockout* fame, was another character referee, who would look out of place with today's robotic refs. He had a run-in with Clown Prince Len Shackleton in a League match at Sunderland.

Len kept querying his decisions to the point where an exasperated Ellis said: 'Listen, Shack, who's refereeing this match – you or me?'

Shack, the wittiest footballer of his generation, countered: 'Neither of us.'

 Arthur refereed the Battle of Berne, the infamous World Cup war between Hungary and Brazil in the 1958 World Cup finals. I asked him if that was his most difficult match, and he told me: 'There was one that gave me a bigger headache, and that was in Coventry in 1956 when Argentinian club champions San Lorenzo were playing in a supposedly friendly match. I had to abandon the game after one of the Argentinian players kicked me after I ordered him off.'

The player was a nineteen-year-old inside-forward called Sanfilippo, and it was said he would never be allowed to kick a ball again after his attack on Ellis. Surprise, surprise, when I played for England against Argentina in the 1962 World Cup finals in Chile their goal in a 3-1 defeat was scored by Sanfilippo. Guess who was playing just behind him? Antonio Rattin, who was to get his marching orders in dramatic circumstances in the 1966 World Cup quarter-final match against England at Wembley.

Arthur, who was like Les Dawson with his humour, told me that in 1953 he went to Argentina with England on a goodwill tour. They played two internationals, one of them unofficial and both refereed by Arthur. In the first game, he gave hotly disputed decisions against England in a match watched by 120,000 spectators including Juan Peron and his wife, Eva.

'England lost 3-1,' said Arthur, 'and the England players were not happy with me. They thought I should have disallowed two of the goals. During the game I was bitten by a mosquito and for the next week I was a yellow colour. I was travelling with the England team and they nicknamed me the Yellow Rat!

'We then played Argentina in a full international, and I had to call the game off after twenty-three minutes because the ground had become waterlogged. The rain was so heavy that I considered calling for lifeboats. As I came off the pitch the Argentinian crowd pelted with me tomatoes and rotten eggs. So not only was I like a drowned, yellow rat but I also stank of bad eggs. England skipper Billy Wright, a good friend, jokingly said I should be put in quarantine.'

 I wonder how Arthur would have handled Jose Mourinho? He may be the special one, but I think the old-timers would have considered him just a mouth on legs.

The following little outburst cost him a five-thousand-pound fine after a Carling Cup semi-final against Manchester United, wrongly suggesting that Alex Ferguson had influenced the referee: 'In the second half it was whistle and whistle, fault and fault, cheat and cheat. The referee controlled the game in one way during the first half but in the second they had dozens of free-kicks. I know the referee did not walk to the dressing rooms alone at half-time.'

The worst referee I ever experienced was when a Spanish ref took charge of our European Cup semi-final second leg against Inter Milan at the San Siro stadium in 1965. Within ten minutes I was saying to Roger Hunt: 'We'll be lucky if this bloody ref gives us a free-kick.'

As the final whistle went we had to physically haul Tommy Smith away from the referee as he attempted to give him the good kicking that he deserved.

Bill Shankly was ashen-faced with anger, and said we had been 'corrupted' to defeat. He told the press to draw their own conclusions about our two perfectly legal goals that were disallowed. I scored one of them and I *know* that it was legal.

Smithy completely lost it at the end and went after the referee, calling him 'El bastido'. He did not book or even warn Tommy.

 All these years on, Saint, and you're still bitter.

 Aye, I am and I'll take my bitterness to the grave. I can take defeat, but I have no doubt in my mind that the ref robbed us of the final and the chance to become the first British winners of the European Cup.

That was the trip when Shanks demanded that they turn the bells off at the monastery near our Lake Como hotel on the eve of the match.

Bob Paisley said, quite reasonably, that they couldn't be expected to stop ringing the bells for a bunch of foreign footballers. Shanks seemed to accept this, but when the next peal started he pleaded with Bob to 'go and tell the head monk to at least muffle them'.

 This is word for word a story told by 1974 FA Cup final referee Gordon Kew: 'It was a bright summer afternoon – the shirt-sleeved and summer-dressed crowd filling the magnificent Sheffield Wednesday stadium at

Hillsborough. They were buzzing with the anticipation of the excitement of the start of another new season. Blue-clad policeman sitting on collapsible stools around the perimeter of the pitch, posses of camera lenses behind the goal, television crews on high. It was the perfect setting for football.

'The preliminaries quickly over, I signalled the kick-off. Within a minute my euphoria was shattered by a roar from the crowd and a strident appeal from the centre-forward: "Are you going to send him for an early bath, ref?"

'What on earth had I missed at such an early stage? Following the centre-forward's outstretched arm and point-ing finger I saw that an apparition had appeared in the centre-circle behind me. Unlike any other footballer I had seen, I made a quick inspection and was able to ascertain that he was certainly of the male species. He was dressed only in thick, horn-rimmed spectacles and hobnailed boots.

'All my refereeing experience and training had not pre-pared me for this.

'A peremptory signal to the nearest policeman and to his inspector by the tunnel brought nothing but a belly laugh and no hint of action.

'Taking my Persil-white handkerchief from my pocket and spreading it wide in my hand, I advanced on the benign transgressor, and with a quick thrust grabbed him by his exposed nether regions.

'Then, in solemn session, we strode to the touchlines, with our images streaming into the television recording system, captured for all time.

'My discomfort was complete when on the following Monday morning I joined my normal commuter train to the City.

'As I entered the carriage, eyes swivelled, fingers pointed and there were distinct sounds of sniggering coming from behind several shielding newspapers.

'In haste I sat down and checked my fly, just in case I was improperly addressed. I opened my newspaper and took refuge behind the sports pages. Then it dawned on me why I was receiving such rapt attention.

'There was a picture of me holding the pitch invader's family jewels in the palm of my hand and covered with just a handkerchief. The headline in thick black type read: "HANKY PANKY KEW"

'I am reliably informed that I am the only male to commit an indecent act with another male on British television and not be charged with it. Had I been I would simply have waved my white handkerchief in surrender.'

 A cricket umpire story now. The legendary fast bowler Harold Larwood once generously agreed to take part in a charity match in the Lancashire League.

It soon became obvious that the umpire was in no mood to give Larwood an inch against the local heroes. After a dead-straight ball rapped the batsman's pad, Larwood made a confident 'How's that?' appeal.

'Not out,' the umpire said.

Larwood bowled again, faster this time, and the batsman slashed at the ball, snicked it, and sent it straight into the wicketkeeper's gloves.

'How's *that*?' called Larwood again, certain that he had got his man.

'Not out,' the umpire said firmly.

Larwood was now really wound up, and with his next ball he unleashed an express delivery that smashed into the wicket, sending the stumps and bails flying.

Larwood then turned to the umpire and said: 'I damned nearly had him that time.'

Tom Graveney, one of the most elegant batsmen I have ever seen, walked out to bat in a Sunday match and was surprised to find the umpire sitting in the members' stand. 'What are you doing there?' asked Tom. 'Shouldn't you be out in the middle?'

'Well, after this lot barracked my last lbw decision,' said the umpire, 'it's obvious you get a better view from here.'

One of the funniest yet at the same time dramatic finishes I ever saw to a match was the World Cup final in 1975. With Australia floundering at 268-9, twenty-three runs short of victory, Dennis Lillee drove a Vanburn Holder delivery straight into the hands of Roy Fredericks at mid-off.

Thinking the Windies had won, the crowd poured on to the pitch – little realising that umpire Tom Spencer had signalled a no-ball.

Fredericks, seeing the batsmen running, tried to throw down the stumps but missed, and the ball disappeared into the invading hordes.

Lillee and his partner Jeff Thomson ran as if their flannels were on fire, completing at least ten runs before the ball was retrieved.

But umpires Dickie Bird and Spencer awarded them just two runs, increased to three under fervent Aussie protests.

The hordes of fans were cleared from the pitch, and Australia were eventually dismissed eighteen runs short and the Windies were crowned world champions.

'Then the invasion started again,' Dickie Bird recalled. 'They grabbed my cap, the boots from the feet of Keith Boyce, Jeff Thomson's pads and all the stumps and bails. But we got the better of them, because we had guessed what was going to happen and so during the tea interval we had swapped them for an old set.'

 Have you noticed, Saint, how umpires have become personality executioners, the way they deliver their dismissal decisions. There is Rudi Koertzen's 'slow death' signal, the left arm rising very slowly up to the sky and back again.

Venkat's 'right-angled' out signal, delivered as if it's almost an after-thought, with the batsman thinking there might still be a chance of him changing his mind.

Steve Bucknor thinks long and hard, then gives a slow

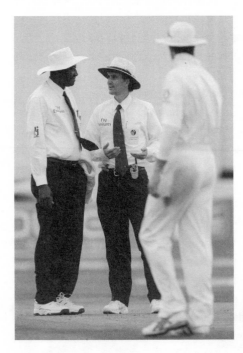

Umpires Steve Bucknor and Billy Bowden, two of cricket's great characters (Jon Super/PA Photos).

nod of the head as the long finger rises, the verdict coming so slowly he would have time to put a black handkerchief on his head as he gives the death penalty.

Then there's the man who seems to be even barmier than Dickie Bird, if that's possible. I refer of course to New Zealand's Billy Bowden, who must have gone to the same School of Funny Walks and Looks as John Cleese. I only discovered while researching for this book that a lot of his odd movements are because he suffers from arthritis, and much of his jigging around is to stop from seizing up. And for all his oddball antics, he is – just like Dickie used to be – a top-class umpire.

 I don't think I could take the verbal stick handed out to tennis umpires. Andy Roddick has taken over from John McEnroe as the main brat of the courts. He smashes so many tennis rackets it's like being at one of The Who's concerts.

He shows little respect to the chair, and calls umpires morons and said to one: 'Have you heard of that part of the body called a spine? Get one!'

Speaking as a Scot, I'm proud of the emergence of Andy Murray as a world-class player. I just hope he concentrates on his tennis rather than the tantrums.

 Murray is out of the McEnroe school, using anger as a form of self-motivation. Being an English gentleman didn't bring Tim Henman any Grand Slams, even with 90 per cent of the Wimbledon crowd willing him on. If it's going to take a few Scottish cuss words from Andy to land the big prizes I guess he's going to have to use the McEnroe abuse method.

Now he's on the vets circuit, Super Mac has to pretend he's still an angry young man to bring in the crowds. He admitted, only half joking: 'These days the promoters dock me a percentage of my appearance money if I don't yell at the umpire and swear as I smash my racket. I guess the fans are paying to see the man I used to be.'

Let's be honest, Saint, he was great to watch in the days when he was yelling at the line judge: 'You cannot be serious, man. *The ball was on the line.*'

Saint's Referee Jokes

The Devil challenges St Peter to a Heaven versus Hell game of football.

St Peter thinks of the calibre of player who has passed through his Gates and realises just by using British players alone he can pick a world-beating side.

He accepts the challenge and then summons the following players: Frank Swift, Alf Ramsey, Roger Byrne, Billy Wright, John Charles, Jim Baxter, Stanley Matthews, Alan Ball, Tommy Lawton, Duncan Edwards, George Best.

The Devil looks over St Peter's shoulder as he is pinning up the team sheet: 'Not a bad line-up,' he admits, 'but how unfortunate for you that I have all the referees.'

* * *

A Premier League referee went to see his doctor because he was concerned that he was getting breathless towards the end of games.

The doctor, who had seen the ref award a match-winning penalty against his Arsenal team at the weekend, told him bluntly: 'Your problem is that you're too fat.'

'No way,' protested the patient. 'I want a second opinion.'

'You asked for it,' said the doctor. 'You're also a crap referee.'

Greavsie's Referee Joke

It's the first day of school and the teacher thought she'd get to know the new children in her class by asking them their name and what their father does for a living.

The first little girl says: 'My name is Daisy and my daddy is a publican.'

The next little boy says: 'I'm Anthony and my dad is an electrician.'

Another boy says: 'My name is Peter, and my father is a bank clerk.'

Then one little boy, wriggling in his seat with embarrassment, says: 'My name is Martin and my father cleans urinals for a living.'

The teacher quickly changes the subject because she senses the boy's humiliation. Later in the school playground she quietly asks Martin if it was really true that his dad cleans urinals for a living, prepared to tell him that he should not feel any shame.

Martin blushes as he confesses: 'No, I'm sorry, my dad doesn't clean urinals. He is a Premier League football referee and I was just too embarrassed to admit it.'

Talk of Football Referees

Gianluca Vialli

In Italy referees either shoot you down with a machine gun or do not blow their whistles at all. In England, referees are amusing.

Jurgen Klinsmann

Before a game I find out the nationality of the referee, and then make sure I swear in a different language to his.

Harry Redknapp

Why can't the fourth official, who is wired up to the referee, have a monitor by the side of the pitch and tell the ref what *really* happened?

David Elleray

In general I am opposed to the use of technology, with perhaps the exception of goal-line issues. I believe that one of the essential attractions of football is that, unlike American football, rugby, cricket, there are very few lengthy stoppages and, for much of the time, it is almost non-stop action. Controversy is also part of the 'enjoyment' of the game – people love arguing/discussing incidents, decisions, etc.

Neil Warnock, commenting on a David Elleray decision:

We were denied the goal by some bald-headed bloke standing fifty yards away.

Jack Taylor, 1974 World Cup final referee:

Refereeing has gone mad. It's all due to the dictates laid down by FIFA. In my day it was me and twenty-two players, it was man management. Now referees have to comply with all the regulations. They have been turned into robots. I was allowed to think for myself, and use some discretion.

Pierluigi Collina, 2002 World Cup final referee:

It angers me when I hear people say that referees are a necessary evil. We are a necessary good. Without us there will be no football.

Bill Shankly

The trouble with referees is that they know the rules but they don't know the game. And there are even some referees who know neither the rules nor the game.

9 THE BEAUTIFUL GAME?

 It is now time for us, Greavsie, to talk about the Beautiful Game.

Which Beautiful Game is that then, Saint? The one being pillaged by a combination of overrated, over-protected, overpaid and over-here mercenaries?

You're an old cynic. You have to admit there are a lot of good things about the game, such as the high level of skill in the Premier League and the superb stadiums and pitches. They make many of the places where you and I played seem like barns, and the pitches were often mud heaps.

I'll concede that the facilities have improved, but you talk to any of the older fans and they'll confirm that the atmosphere is rarely as good as in the good old bad old days. They loved standing on the terraces, and even now with all-seater stadiums many supporters continue to stand.

Saint and Greavsie in Rome with the 1990 World Cup mascot. Saint is telling Greavsie that he looks a prat in that hat (Steve Etherington/PA Photos).

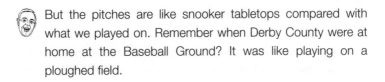 But the pitches are like snooker tabletops compared with what we played on. Remember when Derby County were at home at the Baseball Ground? It was like playing on a ploughed field.

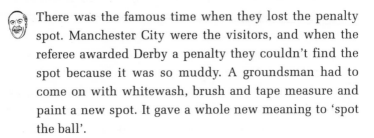 There was the famous time when they lost the penalty spot. Manchester City were the visitors, and when the referee awarded Derby a penalty they couldn't find the spot because it was so muddy. A groundsman had to come on with whitewash, brush and tape measure and paint a new spot. It gave a whole new meaning to 'spot the ball'.

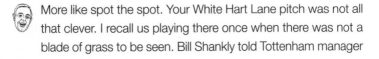 More like spot the spot. Your White Hart Lane pitch was not all that clever. I recall us playing there once when there was not a blade of grass to be seen. Bill Shankly told Tottenham manager

Bill Nicholson: 'You should come and study how we look after our pitch at Anfield. We use *professional* grass.'

Anyway, Jim, if we're going to be Grumpy Old Footballers knocking the foreign imports I think we should have the balls to say which of them we consider the worst buys.

 Okay, Saint, I'm ready to play the game, but for the sake of any legal eagles licking their lips and thinking they might trouser some juicy libel fees let me point out on behalf of the two of us that these are our *opinions*.

Let's go for the top ten 'Worst Premier League Buys'. You have first pick . . .

 Up on Merseyside we still fall about laughing over Everton's signing of Danish central defender **Per Kroldrup**. They bought him from Udinese in June 2005 for just over five million pounds.

He became known as the Invisible Man, because few Everton fans ever saw him. And those who did see him quickly nick-named him Per Cockup. His one Premier League appearance was when Aston Villa thrashed Everton 4-0 on Boxing Day 2005.

It's said that manager David Moyes nearly got lockjaw watching him play, because he was so often open-mouthed in astonishment. Cockup, sorry, Kroldrup stumbled around the pitch like a novice and his attempts to head the ball led to suggestions that Douglas Bader could have done a better job.

Moyes quickly offloaded him to Fiorentina. Everton fans gain brownie points if they can claim: 'I saw Kroldrup play.'

 Newcastle supporters will be quick to agree with me that one of the worst ever buys was the Spanish forward **Albert Luque**. He cost the Magpies £9.5 million in a transfer that was the talk of Tyneside.

His astronomical wages – £85,000 a week – made him the highest paid layabout in football history. He spent more time being pampered on the Newcastle treatment table than on the pitch.

Luque came to St James' Park as a striker, and did a great job of laying down his tools. He made just six Premier League starts in two years before slinking off to Holland for a cut-price £1.5 million. The Geordie fans considered him Luque-warm.

 Your old club Tottenham caught a cold when they signed **Sergei Rebrov** from Dynamo Kiev for a whacking £11.5 million. He had looked outstanding when playing alongside his Ukrainian mate Andriy Shevchenko, but once he got to White Hart Lane he looked as lost as Laurel without Hardy.

In nearly four seasons with Spurs he managed only ten goals in sixty League appearances, and spent much of his time keeping the subs' bench warm. Alan Sugar was club chairman when Rebrov joined, and should have told him: 'You're fired.'

 When Leeds bought **Tomas Brolin** from Parma for £4.3 million somebody likened him to me, and I agreed with the assessment. After all, I am fourteen stone and can hardly raise a gallop.

He had been a cracking player with the Swedish international team, but by the time he got to Elland Road he had begun to pile on the pounds. He managed four goals in nineteen League appearances for Leeds before arriving at Crystal Palace looking like one of the Roly Polies.

 Aston Villa threw away the little matter of £5.8 million on Croatian forward **Bosko Balaban**. He did not start a single League game in his two and a half years at Villa Park, and in

Tomas Brolin, who was weighed down at Leeds (John Marsh/PA Photos).

his seven substitute appearances failed to get a sniff of a goal.

Bosko had been bought to increase Villa's firepower. All he shot was blanks, and he was eventually shipped out on a free transfer just to get him off the payroll. But in fairness, he did decorate the Villa substitutes' bench nicely. The Villa fans composed a fitting alliterative chant for him: 'Bosko Balaban – what a load of bollocks.'

 Fulham forked out £11.5 million of Mohamed Al-Fayed's money for Frenchman **Steve Marlet**. They would have been better off spending the cash in a Harrods sale.

Chris Coleman inherited him when he became manager

at Craven Cottage, and quickly let him go off on loan rather than put up with Marlet's moods and lack of goal power. Supposedly one of the finest strikers in Europe, his Premier League output for Fulham was eleven goals in fifty-four matches. Al Fayed did not need a Harrods cash register to work out that he had cost Fulham £1 million a goal.

 Andrea Silenzi was the first Italian to play in the Premier League, and arguably the worst. Nottingham Forest bought him from Torino in 1995 for what was then by their standards a colossal fee of £1.8 million. Built like Peter Crouch but playing more like Charlotte Church, he failed to find the net in his seven League starts. Andrea is a girl's name over here, which was a fact not lost on the Forest fans who said he played like a big girl.

Forest tore up his contract rather than continue to pay any more wages after he had cost them – with fee and salary – around £3 million. Even Robin Hood didn't get away with that sort of loot when he was at a Nottingham forest.

 Never in the field of football conflict has one man been paid so much for so little as **Winston Bogarde** while with Chelsea. He played eleven matches in four and a half years at Stamford Bridge, collecting a weekly wage of £40,000 while Chelsea were doing everything to get the defiant Dutchman off their books.

Bogarde saw his contract through to the end, accepting the humiliation of being made to train with the reserves and youth team. He wrote a book about his experiences called *Deze Neger Buigt Voor Niemand,* which is double Dutch to me, but I am informed translates as *This Negro Bows for No One.*

The Chelsea accountants reckon they would have been better off signing the late Dirk Bogarde.

 Juan Sebastian Veron cost Man United £28.1 million in July 2001 and they could not wait to pass him on to Chelsea for a cut-price £15 million two years later. For a player of his enormous skill, he was a disaster at Old Trafford and Stamford Bridge.

It made no sense to me when Chelsea moved in for him after he had so obviously failed to settle to the pace of Premier League football with United. In return for their money Chelsea got just seven full Premier appearances – a little over £2 million a match.

 I have to return to Newcastle for the last of our top ten worst buys. Let's be honest, Saint, there could be half a dozen ex-Newcastle players in our list. They have made a procession of abysmal moves into the transfer market.

The player who gets my vote is **Marcelino**, known to Newcastle fans as 'the lesser-spotted Magpie' – because he was seen so few times on the pitch. He managed to play just nineteen Premier League matches in more than three years at St James' Park. One of the reasons for missing so many matches was a broken finger. Geordies gave him the finger when he finally moved back to Spain in 2002. He cost £5 million from Real Madrid. You talk to any Newcastle fan and they wouldn't give tuppence for him.

 These days, Greavsie, Marcelino works as a scout for Liverpool. I just hope he's better at spotting talent than he was at showing it at Newcastle.

While we're in list-making mood, let's – just for a laugh –

select our top ten funniest moments in football. You kick off this time . . .

 Tosh Chamberlain has to be in the list. He was a character who could have stepped out of *Only Fools and Horses* and was always good for a laugh, not always intentionally. Playing for Fulham at Leyton Orient, he stepped up to take a corner kick and managed to miss the ball and kicked the corner stick so hard it broke in two. Johnny Haynes, his captain and best friend, fell on the floor laughing, and was booked for calling him a silly c***. It was Tosh who hit a back pass so hard that it broke the ribs of his goalkeeper Tony Macedo, and he once went on strike during a game 'until I get an apology from the referee . . . that last tackle could have killed me'.

 My first story doesn't involve anything on the pitch but a team talk before a crucial Liverpool–Man United game by the one and only Bill Shankly. I have heard people telling many different versions of the story, but this is the real one. I know, because I was there. I can remember the eve-of-game team talk word for word . . .

Shanks stood by a table that had Subbuteo-type players laid out in team formation. He held up the goalkeeper: 'This', growled Shanks, 'is Alex Stepney . . . Christ, he couldn't catch a cold . . . and he's as frightened of crosses as Count Dracula.' 'Alex' was thrown to one side.

He then held up the figures representing fullbacks Shay Brennan and Tony Dunne. 'Ye've no doubt heard that Matt Busby has got a bad back. Well, let me tell ye that he's got TWO bad backs. They cannae mark time.' Brennan and Dunne were tossed aside.

Shanks was now holding Pat Crerand aloft. 'Aye, he can play if you let him have the ball,' he said. 'So starve him, and remember that's he's the slowest thing on two feet. I've seen milk turn faster.'

Next up for ridicule was Nobby Stiles. 'I've got a garden gnome bigger than this wee fellow,' said Shanks. 'And at least my gnome can see. Stiles is as blind as a bat, so you can easily get past him.' Nobby went flying.

Now he had centre-half Bill Foulkes in his hand, and he flourished it towards me. 'You, laddie, can get a hat-trick against

They managed to enjoy their football: Bill Shankly, Bob Paisley and Tommy Docherty (PA Photos).

him. He's nearly old enough to be your father, and he moves about as quickly as an old age pensioner.'

There were five forwards standing. He picked up John Aston and David Sadler and tossed them on the pile of discarded players. Left on the table were just the Big Three – Bobby Charlton, Denis Law and George Best.

Shanks looked intently around the room at all of us. He indicated the remaining figures with a disdainful sweep of the hand: 'Now you're not going to tell me ye can't beat a three-man team . . .'

While it was hilarious, Shankly was cleverly getting home the point that Charlton, Law and Best should take our main concentration.

If you look up the record books you'll find we won that match at Old Trafford 2-1, just a month before Man United won the European Cup at Wembley.

 Bet you'll remember this, Saint – the day it rained goals. The BBC newsreader wondered if somebody was playing a joke on him when he was handed the First Division results to announce on the afternoon of Boxing Day 1963. There were ten games played, and this is how they finished – reading them in my best BBC announcer voice:

Blackpool 1, Chelsea 5
Burnley 6, Manchester United 1
Fulham 10, Ipswich Town 1
Leicester City 2, Everton 0
Liverpool 6, Stoke City 1
Nottingham Forest 3, Sheffield United 3
Sheffield Wednesday 3, Bolton Wanderers 0
West Bromwich Albion 4, Tottenham Hotspur 4
West Ham United 2, Blackburn Rovers 8
Wolves 3, Aston Villa 3

It went down in football folklore as the day the game went Christmas crackers. There were sixty-six goals scored in the ten matches, and three players – Graham Leggat for Fulham, Andy Lochhead for Burnley and your old sidekick Roger Hunt for Liverpool – helped themselves to four goals each.

The craziest game was at Craven Cottage, where Ipswich took a ten-goal battering from a Fulham side that had England internationals Johnny Haynes, Alan Mullery, George Cohen and a stylish, upright midfield player called Bobby Robson in no mood to show Christmas charity.

But it was a Scot – international centre-forward Graham Leggat – who did most to make the Ipswich defenders look like a gathering of repentant Scrooges determined to give away goals galore for Christmas.

Graham, later the Voice of Football on Canadian television, netted four goals and could easily have doubled his score during a match in which Fulham were made to look like world-beaters.

Yet Ipswich, League champions the previous year, managed to laugh away the heaviest defeat in their history.

The late, much-mourned John Cobbold, their eccentric chairman, said afterwards with typical wit: 'Our problem was our goalkeeper was sober. The rest of us, myself included, were nursing Christmas Day hangovers.'

 Ah, John Cobbold. They don't make them like him any more. He was an Old Etonian who always greeted us like his closest friends when we arrived to play at Portman Road. I remember when they were at the bottom of the table and the newspapers were saying they had a crisis. 'Crisis? What crisis?' he said mockingly. 'A crisis at Ipswich, dear boy, is when the white wine is served at room temperature.'

He once arrived back at Ipswich station after a skiing holiday and went to the front of the train and gave the driver his skis. 'Well,' he said. 'You always tip a taxi driver, so why not a train driver?'

 Right, back to our list. I wish I'd been there to see this one – the United States trainer raced on to the pitch to treat an injured player during the 1930 World Cup semi-final against Argentina. He stumbled and dropped his box of medical supplies and a bottle of chloroform smashed on the pitch.

The trainer took the fumes full in the face as he bent to pick up the box. He folded slowly to the ground like a puppet that has had its strings cut, and he had to be carried back to the touchline bench.

 Bet you didn't know this, Saint – Alex Villaplane proudly captained France in the first ever World Cup finals match in 1930. Fifteen years later the same Alex Villaplane was shot by French resistance fighters for collaborating with the Nazis during the Second World War. It's not my funny story, but I just thought you'd find it interesting in a 'not a lot of people know that' way.

And I don't think you'll be amused by my next story. Scotland suddenly became the team without a manager when Andy Beattie announced his resignation after the Scots had gone down 1-0 to Austria in their opening match of the 1954 finals. Beattie felt he was not being allowed to manage by the Scottish selectors, the equivalent of rugby's Old Farts.

With the interfering selectors in charge, the Scots were beaten 7-0 by Uruguay on a scorching hot day in their final match of the tournament. Right-half Tommy Docherty said:

'We got such a run-around that we were suffering from sunburned tongues.'

 Thanks for shaking that skeleton, Greavsie. It was the first World Cup match screened live on Scottish television, and I remember wanting to kick the nine-inch screen in.

Wee Alan Ball was full of funny stories. He told me of the day he was leaving Goodison in a hurry to join the England squad for a summer tour during his days as an idol at Everton. He was holding a suitcase in either hand, and was confronted by an Everton supporter.

"Ere, Al pal, gi's yer autograph,' the fan said in thick Scouse as he held a blank piece of paper under Ballie's nose.

'Can't you see I've got my hands full?' said Ballie, desperate to catch a train.

The late great Alan Ball with Greavsie (PA Photos).

'Don't worry, Al pal,' said the fan. 'Just spit on the paper. That'll do me.'

As you'll know, Greavsie, when Alf Ramsey first selected Norman 'Bites Yer Legs' Hunter for an England team to meet Spain in Madrid, Ballie called for hush in the dressing room. He then put his hands together and said with bowed head: 'For what they are about to receive . . .'

 We can't have a collection of funny stories without including the one and only George Best, the greatest British player of all time. He once went through an entire game in which, to win a bet, he played the ball only with his left foot. In another match, he passed the ball only to teammate David Sadler, who was playing in the middle of the Man United defence at the time. 'David had moaned at me before the match that I never passed the ball to him,' said George. 'He was sick to death of receiving it by the time the game was over.'

 There was a time in the late 1960s when Everton had two Newtons on their books, Henry and Keith. In their pre-match tactical talk before facing Everton, the West Bromwich Albion players were told to attack Henry Newton on his left side. 'He hasn't got a left foot and so when he's in possession force him on his left all the time,' the coach stressed.

West Brom's Graham Lovett was the first to be tested by an aggressive run from Newton, and he expertly jockeyed him out to the left, making sure he was unable to switch the ball to his right foot.

Then suddenly Newton let fly with a rocketing left foot shot from twenty yards that was a goal from the moment he connected. It was a cracker.

Lovett looked to the touchline bench with his arms opened

wide to express his astonishment. 'Thought you said he only had a right foot!' he shouted.

Back came the reply: 'It's the wrong bloody Newton . . .!'

The goalscorer was KEITH Newton, England international fullback and a left-foot specialist.

 Two of the funniest goals I scored both involved outstanding goalkeepers. The first was in a League game for Tottenham against Fulham at Craven Cottage. Their goalie was Tony Macedo, who was born in Gibraltar and while usually reliable could sometimes become a crumbling rock at the back of the Fulham defence.

Tony had been to see the Harlem Globetrotters giving a basketball exhibition a couple of days before our match. As he collected the ball early in the game, he started to give an impersonation of the Globetrotters. He ran round the penalty area bouncing the ball and crouched in the style of Meadowlark Lemon, the star Globetrotters dribbler.

Inspired by the cheers of the crowd, Tony mimed Meadowlark-style as if to throw the ball to an opponent – me, standing unmarked on the edge of the penalty area. He switched his aim to Fulham skipper Johnny Haynes, but the ball slipped out of his hand and landed at my feet. All I had to do was side-foot the ball into the empty net.

I couldn't resist shouting to Tony: 'You silly basket.' What Johnny Haynes called him is unprintable!

My other story features my old mate Gordon Banks. He was in goal for Leicester against Tottenham at White Hart Lane, and we were awarded a penalty just before half-time.

The pitch was a mud heap, and as I placed the ball on the spot Gordon went into the back of the net to wipe his palms on a patch of dry grass. As he bent down I jokingly slid the ball into the other corner of the net. I don't know who was more amazed when the referee awarded a goal.

As I laughed with my Tottenham team-mates all the way back to the centre-circle Gordon raced after the referee and gave him a real mouthful, for which he got booked. That really rubbed it in.

 Two unforgettable football characters feature in our last story, Alan Ball and Bill Shankly, both of them sadly now gone to the great football stadium in the sky.

There have been scores of stories told about Shanks. One of my favourites was passed on to me by Ballie, who recalled: 'I had been booked by referee Clive "The Book" Thomas during a Mersey derby for a tackle on Ian Callaghan. Shanks told me afterwards that he didn't think the tackle warranted a booking, and he generously said that he would give evidence for me if I wanted to appeal. This was really big of him, the Liverpool manager speaking up for an Everton player. The hearing was in London, and Shanks came down with Chris Lawler, who had to appear before the committee about a booking in another match.

'Chris was first in and his appeal was kicked out, despite a plea on his behalf by Shanks. Then it was my turn to be called before the committee. There was a game of table football set out on the board in front of the officials so that people involved could move the little plastic figures around to show what had happened.

'First Clive Thomas and his two linesmen gave their version of my tackle. One of the linesmen had his evidence dismissed because the committee felt he was too far away from the incident.

'Then I gave evidence and called Ian Callaghan as my first witness. He said that he thought that my tackle had been a fair one.

'Next I called Shanks, which was the cue for some hilarious exchanges that could have come from a Carry On film.

'"Please describe the incident to us, Mr Shankly," said the committee chairman.

'"Certainly, sir," said Shanks in his Scottish growl of a voice. "But first I want to say that the witness in Chris Lawler's case was a bloody liar."

'The chairman moved uncomfortably in his seat. "Quite, Mr Shankly," he said. "But that case is closed. Can you please confine your comments to this case."

'Shanks delivered one of those looks of his that could turn rock to jelly. Then he gave a full account of how he had witnessed my tackle and he paused and looked hard at the committee members before saying: "I'm as astonished as I was with Chris Lawler that this wee laddie was booked for an innocuous tackle."

'He added: "It was perfectly fair in this man's game of ours and did not warrant a booking – just like Chris Lawler did not deserve to have his name taken."

'"Yes," said the chairman, wearily. "You have made your point about the Lawler case. Can we please establish just how clearly you saw Ball's tackle on Callaghan."

'"I saw it clearly from my position in the dug-out," said Shanks. "I saw it as clearly as I can see you gentlemen."

'Clive Thomas jumped in with what he considered a relevant point. "You say you were sitting in the dug-out, Mr Shankly."

'"Aye, I was," said Shanks. "You know that's where I always sit. It's like my second home."

'"Well, one of my linesmen," said Thomas, "has had his evidence dismissed because it was considered he was too far away from the incident. Yet he was standing on the touchline in front of the dug-out at the time. How could you have possibly seen it if you were behind him?"

'The referee appeared to have made a good point in true Perry Mason style. But Shanks was never beaten that easily in his life.

'Back he came with the reply: "I saw the incident developing, so I stood up and threw the linesman to one side. It meant I had a clear unobstructed view of what was about to happen."

'The whole room shook with laughter. This was Shanks at his most outrageous and I just wish television cameras had been there to capture it.

'As he left the room, he growled over his shoulder: "And there's no way that Chris Lawler deserved to be booked."'

Ballie lost his case, but collected a priceless story that he was able to tell for years afterwards.

 Shanks and Ballie, two of the greatest characters the game has ever known. Can you imagine how competitive they're being Up There, Saint? Neither of them would ever concede an inch during their football careers. With so many frauds around these days, how our football could do with their attitude, desire and determination today . . . and also their humour.

Saint's Football Joke

Mohamed Al-Fayed summons all of Fulham's forwards to an emergency meeting in the Harrods boardroom.

He instructs them to watch the cinema-size screen that slides down to a centre position on the wall. An IT man inserts a DVD and for the next hour the Fulham players sit and watch a documentary on the world's great explorers.

They see Sir Ranulph Fiennes at the South Pole, Sir Edmund Hillary at the top of Everest, Neil Armstrong taking the first giant step on to the Moon, and the astronauts working in the space Skylabs.

Al-Fayed then addresses the players. He waves the club accounts in their direction. 'I pay each of you here around £60,000 a week . . . A WEEK!' he says.

'Now which of you idiots can explain why the great explorers and adventurers we have been watching can explore the Antarctic, reach the Moon, scale Everest and search the universe . . . and yet not one of you can find your way into the f****** penalty area?'

Greavsie's Football Joke

The Premier League manager and his wife of twenty years were lying in bed. He was reading the Saint's auto-biography and she was half-concentrating on a crossword, with a wandering mind.

'Darling,' she said, looking up from her crossword.

'Um?' he replied, engrossed in the Saint's riveting story.

'If I died would you get married again?' she asked.

Wondering if this was a trick question, he thought for a moment before answering. 'I don't see why not,' he said. 'Our marriage has been a happy one and you'd want me to be happy again, wouldn't you?'

'Yes, I suppose,' she answered.

They continued in silence for a while, the husband going back to his book and his wife giving floating con-centration to her crossword.

'Darling,' she started again.

'Um?' he replied, a little irritated to have his reading interrupted again.

'If you got married again, would you let your new wife wear my dresses?'

He put his book down and gently took her hand. Again realising this was a loaded question with no satis-factory answer, he thought for a moment and said, 'I guess I would. After all, it would be a shame just to throw away those nice clothes of yours in which you look so wonderful.'

They lapsed back into silence, he returning to his book and she doodling with a pencil on the crossword grid.

'Darling,' she once again started.

'Um?' he replied, wondering what was coming next.

'Would you let her wear my shoes?'

This time he did not even look up from his book as he responded: 'Yes, and for the same reason. It would be a shame to throw away all your expensive shoes.'

They lapsed back into silence, the husband reading and the wife getting into a more depressed mood as she absent-mindedly shaded in the white squares on the crossword grid.

'Darling,' she said. 'Would you let her have my seat in the directors' box?'

'Well, my love, we wouldn't want to have an empty seat right next to the chairman, would we,' he said after careful thought. 'So, yes, I would let her sit in your seat.'

'Honey,' she said, continuing the inquisition.

'Um?' he replied.

'Would you let her use my new golf clubs?'

Without hesitation, he answered, 'Of course not, she's left-handed.'

Talk of Old Footballers (The way it was)

Bill Shankly, advising the Saint:

Look, laddie, if you're in the penalty area and aren't quite sure what to do with the ball, just stick it in the net and we'll discuss all your options afterwards.

Brian Clough, sitting on the fence as usual with his opinion of Sports Minister Colin Moynihan:

Have you ever seen anybody like him in your bloody life? I'd like to grab him by the balls and strangle him.

Jim Baxter

When Charlie Cooke sold you a dummy you had to pay to get back into the ground.

Stan Bowles

I look at some of the people around today and I bloody well weep. They're talking about spending millions on these players, and the poor blokes can't play the game. Can't trap a dead rat, yet they're making a fortune. Good luck to them, I suppose. I'm going to the betting shop to take my anger out on the gee-gees.

Rodney Marsh, greeting Gordon Jago as new QPR manager:

Good luck, boss. We're all behind you fifty per cent.

Graeme Souness

If they had used video evidence in my day I would still be doing time.

Bobby Robson

We shall set out to be as positive as possible and look to pick up a point.

Tommy Docherty, on Welsh international winger Leighton James:

He's very deceptive. He's even slower than he looks.

Danny Blanchflower

The FA Cup final is a great occasion, but only until ten minutes before the kick-off. Then we players come on and ruin the whole thing.

Allan Clarke, interviewed by Brian Moore while at Leeds:

I don't think, Brian. You don't think in this game.

Billy Wright, on his infamous missed tackle against Ferenc Puskas in England's first defeat at Wembley:

Puskas went this way and I went that way. *Times* reporter Geoffrey Green said that I was like a fire engine going in the wrong direction for the blaze.

Tommy Lawton, on the crossing accuracy of Stanley Matthews:

I've had to give Stanley a telling-off. He was crossing the ball with the lace facing me.

Len Shackleton

I find football an easy game. It's the other players on the pitch who make it hard.

Joe Mercer, to his Man City players after they had scored an own goal following a series of back passes from the opponents' half:

I have been in this game for fifty f****** years and congratulate you on finding a new way to score a f****** goal.

Ron Greenwood

Glenn Hoddle hasn't been the Glenn Hoddle we know, and neither has Bryan Robson.

Johnny Haynes

Sometimes at Fulham you feel as if you're not so much passing the ball as passing the buck.

Sir Alf Ramsey

When a player pulls on the England shirt I expect him to grow with pride, and then do as I say.

Ray Clemence

At times it was so easy playing at the back of that magnificent Liverpool defence that I felt guilty about collecting my wages.

Ian Rush

I just couldn't settle in Italy . . . it was like living in a foreign country.

Mick Lyons

If there was no such thing as football, we'd all be frustrated footballers.

10 THINGS THEY WISH THEY HADN'T SAID

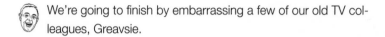
We're going to finish by embarrassing a few of our old TV colleagues, Greavsie.

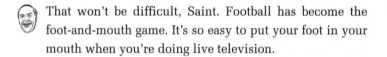
That won't be difficult, Saint. Football has become the foot-and-mouth game. It's so easy to put your foot in your mouth when you're doing live television.

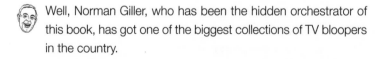
Well, Norman Giller, who has been the hidden orchestrator of this book, has got one of the biggest collections of TV bloopers in the country.

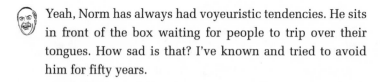
Yeah, Norm has always had voyeuristic tendencies. He sits in front of the box waiting for people to trip over their tongues. How sad is that? I've known and tried to avoid him for fifty years.

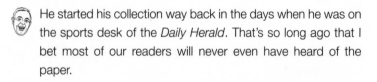
He started his collection way back in the days when he was on the sports desk of the *Daily Herald*. That's so long ago that I bet most of our readers will never even have heard of the paper.

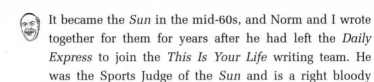 It became the *Sun* in the mid-60s, and Norm and I wrote together for them for years after he had left the *Daily Express* to join the *This Is Your Life* writing team. He was the Sports Judge of the *Sun* and is a right bloody know-all.

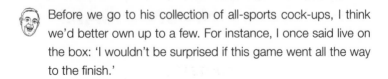 Before we go to his collection of all-sports cock-ups, I think we'd better own up to a few. For instance, I once said live on the box: 'I wouldn't be surprised if this game went all the way to the finish.'

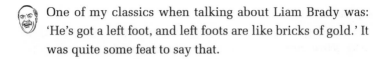 One of my classics when talking about Liam Brady was: 'He's got a left foot, and left foots are like bricks of gold.' It was quite some feat to say that.

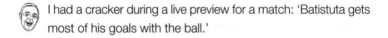 I had a cracker during a live preview for a match: 'Batistuta gets most of his goals with the ball.'

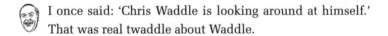 I once said: 'Chris Waddle is looking around at himself.' That was real twaddle about Waddle.

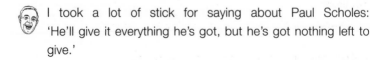 I took a lot of stick for saying about Paul Scholes: 'He'll give it everything he's got, but he's got nothing left to give.'

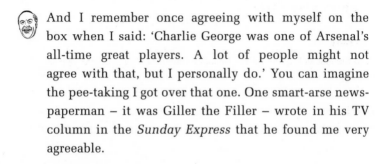 And I remember once agreeing with myself on the box when I said: 'Charlie George was one of Arsenal's all-time great players. A lot of people might not agree with that, but I personally do.' You can imagine the pee-taking I got over that one. One smart-arse news-paperman – it was Giller the Filler – wrote in his TV column in the *Sunday Express* that he found me very agreeable.

I think that's enough about our cock-ups, Greavsie. Here to close our book is a collection of 100 things they wish they hadn't said on TV and radio.

 Anybody who enjoys the list can thank us. Anybody annoyed by it can blame Know-all Norm. They start with a few golden oldies, kicking off with dear old Motty . . .

FOOTBALL

John Motson
For the benefit of those of you watching in black and white, Spurs are wearing the yellow shirts.

Jack Charlton
The players with the wind will have to control it a lot more . . .

Bob Wilson
Charlie George has just pissed a late fartness test.

Frank Bough
The Norwich goal was scored by Kevin Bond, who is the son of his father.

David Coleman, referring to hole-in-the-heart footballer Asa Hartford:
He is a whole-hearted player.

Alan Parry
With the last kick of the game, Malcolm Macdonald has scored with his head.

Barry Davies
The Austrians are wearing the dark-black socks.

David Coleman, an
outstanding broadcaster who
inspired the *Private Eye*
column 'Colemanballs'
(Barratts/PA Photos).

Jimmy Hill

Scotland were unlucky not to get another penalty like the one that wasn't
given in the first half.

John Helm

We're coming to the end of the half, and the referee is looking at his
whistle . . .

Archie MacPherson

There aren't many last chances left for George Best.

Gary Newbon

And there'll be more football in a moment, but first we've got highlights of
the Scottish League Cup final.

Jim Rosenthal

Peter Ward has become a new man, just like his old self.

Gerry Harrison

Larosa is nineteen – that's on his back, that is.

Lawrie McMenemy

I hope Robson doesn't blow up because of the heat.

Gerald Sinstadt

I'm sure that Ron Greenwood will hope that by the time England get to Spain, Kevin Keegan will have got his misses out of his system.

Tommy Docherty

Oldham are leading 1-0, a well-deserved victory at this stage of the game.

Andy Gray

It's one of the greatest goals ever, but I'm surprised that people are talking about it being the goal of the season.

David Pleat

We are now in the middle of the centre of the first half.

Trevor Brooking

He's chanced his arm with his left foot.

Peter Withe

It's an end-of-season curtain raiser.

John Motson

Reinders is standing on the ball with Breitner, and Muller has gone to join them . . .

Brian Moore

. . . and their manager, Terry Neill, isn't here today, which suggests he is elsewhere.

Kevin Keegan

He opened his legs and went pretty quick.

John Motson, a master of the microphone who only occasionally got his tongue in a tangle (Jon Buckle/PA Photos).

Claudio Ranieri

The Stamford Bridge pitch is sh*t, yes very sh*t. But it okay. It OUR sh*t.

Alan Mullery

He's done nothing wrong, but his movement's not great and his distribution's been poor.

Rodney Marsh

I'm not going to pick out anyone in particular, but Jay Jay Okocha should not be the captain of a football club.

Steve Claridge

They've forced them into a lot of unforced errors.

Steve Coppell

The lad got overexcited when he saw the whites of the goalpost's eyes.

Ray Wilkins

Signori has all the tricks up his book.

Anne Robinson, on *The Weakest Link:*

Which 'K' is Britain's most widespread bird of prey?

Geoff Hurst

Eagle.

Phil Neal

The midfield picks itself – Beckham, Gerrard, Scholes and AN Other.

John Motson

The Argentinians are numbered alphabetically.

Denis Law

It was one of those goals that's invariably a goal.

Dave Bassett

The past is history.

Alan Shearer

You only get one opportunity of an England debut.

Arsène Wenger, on contract negotiations with Patrick Vieira:

I have to sit down with Patrick to see where we stand.

Gary Mabbutt

When I say that Alex Ferguson needs to stand up and be counted, I mean that he needs to sit down and take a look at himself in the mirror.

Ally McCoist

Craig Bellamy has literally been on fire this season.

Jimmy Floyd Hasselbaink

Any player who says a goal is better than sex is not having proper sex.

Kenny Dalglish

The Brazilians aren't as good as they used to be, or as they are now.

Ron Atkinson

He could have done a lot better there, but full marks to the lad.

Bobby Robson

If you're going to put me on the fence, I'd say he is the best in Europe.

Ossie Ardiles

Glenn is putting his head in the frying pan.

David Pleat

A game is not won until it's lost.

Jack Charlton

The Arsenal defence is skating close to the wind.

Terry Venables

It's either a penalty or it's not a penalty.

Des Lynam

Sometimes it can be.

Jimmy Hill

Come on, Terry, what chances have Germany got of going through? Don't sit on the fence.

Terry Venables

I think it's fifty-fifty.

Howard Wilkinson

Once Tony Daley opens his legs, you've got a problem.

Pele

I think that France, Germany, Spain, Holland and England will join Brazil in the semi-finals.

Mark Lawrenson

There won't be a dry house in the place.

John Aldridge

The match was a real game of cat and dog.

Terry Venables

If history is going to repeat itself, I think we can expect the same thing again.

Arsène Wenger

Alex Ferguson's only weakness is that he thinks he doesn't have one.

Richard Keys

Well, wasn't that the most nail-biting and dramatic finale?

Alan Shearer

Yeah, especially at the end.

Bryon Butler

Fifty-two thousand people here at Maine Road tonight, but my goodness me, it seems like fifty thousand.

Jimmy Armfield

They have more ability in the middle of the field in terms of ability.

Ron Atkinson

Yes, Woodcock would have scored but his shot was just too perfect.

Billy McNeill

Manchester United have got the bull between the horns now.

Phil Neal

The run of the ball is not in our court at the moment.

Graham Taylor

Do I not like orange.

Jock Wallace

Ian Durrant has grown both physically and metaphorically in the close season.

Martin Tyler

Oh, he had an eternity to play that ball, but he took too long over it.

Alan Green

Well, he had two stabs at the cherry.

Jock Brown

Once again it was Gough who stood firm for Scotland in the air.

Tony Gubba

The scoreline didn't really reflect the outcome.

Jimmy Hill

Manchester United are looking to Frank Stapleton to pull some magic out of the fire.

Alan Parry

A win tonight is the minimum City must achieve.

Terry Neill

I'm not superstitious or anything like that, but I'll just hope we'll play our best and put it in the lap of the gods.

Joe Royle

I don't blame individuals – I blame myself.

Bobby Robson

I do want to play the long ball and I do not want to play the short ball. I think long and short balls is what football is all about.

Yes, Sir Bobby, a load of balls.

OTHER SPORTS

Murray Walker

Do my eyes deceive me, or is Senna's Lotus sounding rough?

Martin Brundle

And Michael Schumacher just stood on his seat and pulled out something special.

Sue Barker

. . . and later we will have action from the men's cockless pairs.

Alan Minter

Sure there have been injuries and deaths in boxing – but none of them serious.

Dennis Pennis

'Have you ever thought of writing your autobiography?

Chris Eubank

On what?

Frank Bruno

You get these sort of things in boxing, 'Arry. That's cricket, old boy.

Harry Carpenter

Magri has to do well against this unknown Mexican who comes from a famous family of five boxing brothers.

Henry Blofeld

In the rear, the small diminutive figure of Shoaib Mohammad who can't be much taller or shorter than he is.

Henry Blofeld again

Paul Allott is the lovely type of chap you want to meet behind the pavilion.

Jim Laker

It's a unique occasion, really – a repeat of Melbourne 1977.

Tony Cosier

Now Botham, with a chance to put everything that's gone before, behind him.

David Acfield

Strangely, in slow motion replay, the ball seemed to hang in the air for even longer.

Peter Alliss

In technical terms, he's making a real pig's ear of it.

Lee Westwood

I'm a golfer – not an athlete.

Ken Brown, discussing Nick Faldo and his caddy Fanny Sunesson:

Some weeks Nick likes to use Fanny; other weeks he prefers to do it by himself.

John Francome

The racecourse is as level as a billiard ball.

David Coleman

This could be a repeat of what will happen next week at the European Athletics Championships.

David Coleman again

Linford Christie's got a habit of pulling it out when it matters most.

'Whispering' Ted Lowe

He's going for the pink – and for those of you with black and white sets, the yellow is behind the blue.

'Whispering' Ted Lowe again

For those of you watching who do not have television sets, live commentary is on Radio 2.

John Virgo

At that pace he was always going to hit it or miss it.

Phil Liggett

Greg LeMond has literally come back from the dead to win the Tour de France.

Brough Scott

When the stalls open, the horses are literally going to explode.

Sid Waddell

The pendulum is swinging back and forth like a metronome.

David Campese

The only thing you're likely to catch on the end of an England three-quarter line is chilblains.

Nigel Starmer-Smith

If you didn't know him, you wouldn't know who he was.

Ray French

. . . and he's got the icepack on his groin there, so possibly not the old shoulder injury.

Pat Glenn, weightlifting commentator:

This is Gregoriava from Bulgaria. I saw her snatch this morning and it was amazing.

David Vine

Here we are in the Holy Land of Israel – a Mecca for tourists.

And finally, from The Master . . .

David Coleman

And the line-up for the final of the women's 400 metres hurdles includes three Russians, two East Germans, a Pole, a Swede and a Frenchman.